Renewing Public Management

An agenda for local governance

Michael Clarke

General Editors:
Michael Clarke and John Stewart

 In association with the
Institute of Local Government Studies

PITMAN PUBLISHING
128 Long Acre, London WC2E 9AN

A Division of Pearson Professional Limited

First published in Great Britain 1996

© Pearson Professional Limited 1996

The right of Michael Clarke to be identified as Author of this Work has been asserted
by him in accordance with the Copyright, Designs and Patents Act 1988.

British Library Cataloguing in Publication Data
A CIP catalogue record for this book can be obtained from the British Library.

ISBN 0 273 61986 1

10 9 8 7 6 5 4 3 2 1

Typeset by Phoenix Photosetting, Chatham, Kent
Printed and bound in Great Britain by Redwood Books, Trowbridge, Wiltshire.

The Publishers' policy is to use paper manufactured from sustainable forests.

Contents

Editors' foreword

This book is one of a series of management handbooks published by Pitman Publishing in association with the Institute of Local Government Studies in the School of Public Policy at the University of Birmingham. The series is designed to help those concerned with management in local government to meet the challenge of the late 1990s. It is based on the belief that no period has been so important for local authorities to have effective management, responsive to both citizen and customer.

The mid 1990s has brought reorganisation to local authorities in Scotland, Wales and parts of England. No local authority, however, can escape the need to keep under continuous review its political and managerial structures and processes. All councils are caught up in far-reaching changes. Some of these come from local determination and decision, others from central government policy and yet others from deeper changes in society. New problems, issues and opportunities demand from local governments a capacity to respond in new ways. They have to become closer in their local communities, their public and the wide range of institutions and organisations involved in the governance of localities; they need to find imaginative solutions to the evermore complex problems of public policy; they have to manage their resources to achieve value for money and value in the services they provide; and they have to achieve effective management in all their activities. These are formidable challenges for the managers — and the politicians — involved.

There are plenty of management books, but this series is distinct. Its starting point is the need for emphasis on developing effective management in local government, associated with the need to take account of the particular nature of local government. The series sets out to be succinct and to be useful in the practical day to day world as well as being designed to be used as a prompt to management improvement.

In no sense are we pretending that this or other books in the series will show a *single way* to manage the local authority. Management is not like that. Our intention is to explore ideas and questions in order to help fashion the most helpful and effective approach to the local situation. We believe that local authority politicians and managers should draw on as wide a range of experience as possible but that this should be set in the context of the special purposes, conditions and tasks of local government. We hope that this book contributes to that end.

Professor Michael Clarke, Head of School of Public Policy
University of Birmingham

Professor John Stewart, Institute of Local Government Studies
in the School of Public Policy, University of Birmingham

1

Introduction: vision and reality

Local government is undergoing enormous change. It has been doing so for a decade and more. These are almost truisms. Yet, in the middle of the changes it is often difficult to see what is going on — as we stagger from one crisis or 'challenge' to another. From the outside it all looks complicated and perplexing. The reality is that the changes are profound, shifting not just the way in which local government's work is done from day to day, but also its basic nature, role and relationships. This has all manner of implications for a wide range of people.

This book is written to try and help sort out the important implications. So it is written for a number of different audiences. The first, and most obvious, group is the managers working within the traditional framework of local government. If anyone truly owns the agenda set out in the pages which follow, it is them. The second group is those who are elected as councillors to represent their communities and to lead and shape the work of the local authority. They are second, not because they are less important but because of their role. They play a key part in management, particularly at a strategic level, but do not have the same kind of involvement in the day-to-day life of the organisation as their officers. One of the themes of the agenda is about getting the respective contributions and relationships of officers and members right and the importance for members of being clear about their role and responsibilities.

A conventional book about local government management might well stop there. The essence of this book is that there should be a bigger audience. One of its arguments is that the increasingly common use of the term 'local governance' is no accident. One of the big changes which has happened has been a shift in reality and perception. The new reality is that there is an increased number of organisations and agencies — and thus people — taking part in the government of our localities. The shift in perception is the

1

recognition of this and the realisation that, while it is not new, it requires new focus and attention.

Thus, although the book starts from a local government perspective, it is relevant to a third audience — the whole range of people in other parts of the public sector, in the voluntary sector and in the private sector who find themselves drawn into the governance of their locality and thus into the web of local public management. Many of these people are themselves having to sort out how they relate to one another and what it is they are being called on to do.

There is then an ever-widening circle of people around these central actors. There is a range of local opinion-formers, critics, observers and occasional participants in local governance who may be frustrated, perplexed, intrigued, excited or, even, just mildly interested in what is going on. While the book is not written to describe or explain the workings of the system to the outsider, it should provide some useful insights to those who have some investment in the way their locality is governed. It will give them a feel for the key issues which are being grappled with by those on the inside. Finally, and beyond the locality, there are students of (local) government for whom this book will provide another perspective in their studies.

❏ Vision . . .

A book like this could well set out a vision of what local government — and local governance — might be like. A vision is useful in that it can provide a framework for thinking about the present and its improvement, but it can also be a distraction, providing a means of escape from dealing with the realities of the present. Most of us will have a vision, or element of one. For most of us such a vision will include such things as:

- a better understood and defined role in community leadership;
- a different kind of central – local relationship;
- greater fiscal autonomy for local government;
- a different approach to political management, perhaps with a changed balance between political leadership (however expressed) and a deliberative or 'legislative' council;
- stronger identity and ownership by citizens of their local government and more involvement;

- an electoral system based on proportional representation;

- reconciliation of some of the dilemmas in the contemporary situation, i.e. between an entrepreneurial approach and integrity and equity; between flexibility and responsiveness, and fairness and consistency; between clarity of direction and the diversity of a plural local society; and so on.

For each of us our vision will be tempered by our experience and circumstances although vision needs to be set beyond the bounds of present reality.

However much a vision informs our approach, reality *will* be different. For anyone involved in local government or local governance there is obligation to make reality better. This should be about trying to move towards the vision, but the vision must not be allowed to impede. Immediate improvements must not be put off just because they are not the ideal!

This book is about that process. Its author has a vision of what things could be like, and some of that probably shows through the text, but the book is about improving things as they stand. In this, it is not a justification for what is or has been. It is, rather, an argument that, within the present, there are important things to be done.

It is published at a time when significant shifts have taken and are taking place. It may not yet be clear precisely where these are leading nor what happens next. Some will yearn for the return to what they see as a golden past and a more powerful (controlling?) local government. Others will welcome the recognition of a more plural local governance, but want to find ways of strengthening and clarifying local government's role and the local capacity to focus and integrate. But that is more to do with dealing with reality.

❏ . . . and reality

The realities of *local government* (which will be taken to be the traditional framework and institutions of the local authority) and *local governance* (which will be defined as the process through which shape and direction are given to our localities and public choices made and priorities set for the provision and services which underpin them) are complex. The impact of a whole range of changes — legislative and more general — on local government and its direct involvement in the locality is transforming the way it works and challenging and re-shaping many of the conventions and assumptions which have marked its recent history. A familiar world has gone. Many of those managing the corporate centre, the services or the regulatory responsibilities of the local authority work in largely uncharted territory.

Even if it is over-simplifying, the local government of old could be thought of as not just important but largely autonomous, operating with a high degree of self-sufficiency in more or less monopoly circumstances. The contemporary situation is very different. We shall explore the points in more detail, but:

- the emergence of mixed economies of providers;
- the growth of 'partnership' activity of various sorts;
- the increasing number of special purpose agencies;
- increased differentiation (some would say fragmentation) within public service organisations (particularly within local government itself and in the NHS);
- more and more policy problems which show no respect for organisational and sector boundaries;
- and an increasingly diverse and plural society

all require us to re-define the situation. There is a high degree of inter-dependence between agencies and a complexity which, if not new, is much greater than it was. The implications for skills and competences, style and approach, and ways of working are enormous. While they are obviously real for local authority managers, they also spill over into the life of all those people and organisations involved in local governance. Indeed, part of what is going on is a re-definition of local public management. The agenda set by this book should help that process.

The search for good management anywhere demands an understanding of the circumstances and environment within which it takes place. It also demands some sense of priority about the key issues to be tackled. Inevitably the peculiar circumstances which confront any organisation or any locality will set their own constraints and opportunities. Thus the agenda which is presented here can only provide a framework. It is generalised and not specific. Its utility will be in helping to keep sight of the wood as well as the trees. In the middle of change and rapidly shifting events it is often difficult to discern direction and sort out what is important.

❏ Public management

While the agenda — and thus the book — is about finding ways of managing better, two notes of caution should be sounded from the beginning. The first concerns the limitations of management; the second is about fashion. Good public management is an important ingredient of good government — local or national. The need to search for improvement and to maintain a critical approach to the way it is conducted can be taken as a *sine qua non*. However, good management is not enough. Management is not an end in itself, it is a means to an end.

Good management is no substitute for sound, substantial policy designed to achieve well-defined ends; or for getting right the instruments which will translate policy into practice; or for the process of delivery or implementation. It is, rather, the enabling of each of them. That should be obvious, yet so much of what is said and written about management leaves an impression that if you get *it* right everything else will follow. There is a balance to be achieved — it is that which has to be got right.

But there is more than that. In the public domain, management takes place within a framework of public debate, characterised by conflicting values and interests, public choice, public accountability and a political environment (however immediate or distant the relationship between manager and politician). Good *public* management thus has to work within this framework and be sensitive to it. This may also seem an obvious point but it is one worth making explicit. Managers need to be clear about the implications. We have come through a period when management in the private sector was seen to be the model and hold all the answers; we now need to properly rediscover public management — and to be clear when we can learn from elsewhere.

Good though this sounds it is not simple. Local governance and thus local public management involves people who are in the voluntary and private sectors as well as the public sector. Two immediate points about this. On the one hand, we need to avoid making simplistic 'public' and 'private' distinctions and recognise the blurred boundaries between sectors. On the other, all those involved need to share in the task of re-defining what it means and its practical implications — hence the third audience for this book.

The point about fashion is straight-forward, but telling. Fashion in terms of ideas, concepts, approaches, techniques and so on plays an important part in management. There is nothing necessarily wrong in this — particularly if it causes managers to search, question and think of new ways of doing things. The problem is that, too often, there is something deeper. It is tempting to want to believe that there are quick, simple and universal solutions to complex and difficult problems. The latest fashion is thus often embraced too easily and great faith invested in its potential. The crown, of course, usually proves to be hollow.

In setting this agenda and pointing to a range of issues to be tackled and ideas to be pursued there is no suggestion that there are quick-fixes or easy solutions. Managing public organisations and public policy is as complicated and complex as any kind of management — more so if anything. Changing organisations, creating new structures and processes, shifting people's attitudes and nurturing new skills and behaviours is a time-consuming and slow business. There are no simple models and it does not happen overnight, whatever the rhetoric may suggest.

❑ Continued renewal not re-invention

The language of 're-invention' has crept into the fashionable vocabulary: just as we have heard much of supposed management 'revolution' in local government as a result of the changes of the 1980s and 1990s. This language is misleading. It suggests that there was a single paradigm of public management and that, for some reason, we have moved to a new one. Neither is right. There always have been mixtures of models and approaches; this will continue. Moreover, change will also continue. There is no reason to believe that we have moved through a period of massive upheaval to a new stability. If we are seriously interested in improving local public management and the performance of local governance, the language of evolution and continued renewal is more appropriate. There is no doubt that there has been large scale transformation; this book argues the need for further transformation. Circumstances will shift, new ideas will develop and so yet further transformation will be needed.

The reason for this book should now be evident. We are in the middle of enormous changes whose thrust and direction may not always be clear; there is a need to understand them as best we can and to test out their implications. Whatever the unique role and responsibilities of local government as such, it is only part of the wider process of local governance; the changes affecting local councils and the strategic and operational requirements for local governance throw up a formidable array of challenges and opportunities. The demands of the public, with its plurality of interests and values, add their own particular momentum and imperatives.

❑ The agenda

The agenda which emerges is not exhaustive. It could not be; but it provides a base for individual managers and organisations to think through where they are and establish what they need to consider doing.

Chapter 2 summarises the agenda set out in the chapters which follow. Chapter 3 looks at the principal threads of change, provides a backcloth to the discussion by extending debate about some of the issues flagged in this introduction and asserts the importance of thinking about local governance and a different kind of local public management. In Chapter 4 political leadership, the changing political management of local government, its relationships to other leaderships and the framework of local governance and the importance of democracy and how the plurality of local society is best reflected, are explored.

Chapter 5 goes on to look at the strategy, purpose and direction, the need for an holistic approach and for making horizontal connections across policy and operations, the place of research and intelligence, the role of the strategic centre and the importance of putting management into its wider context. Organisational issues are pursued in Chapter 6, which looks at the need to match organisation to purpose, the management of differentiation, sorting out what management is, developing both organisation and management and recognising the particular demands of working across organisational boundaries and in the community. Chapter 7 moves from a top-down approach to remind us of the need to be closer to people; it looks at decentralisation and the business of 'letting go' with its implications for sharing power; relations between levels of local government and with different kinds of community; service relationships with users; and the structures and processes needed to sustain all of this together with the implications for skills, style and approach.

In Chapter 8 the new world of service management is explored, focusing on the commissioning role of the local authority, the need to be clear about means of implementation and delivery, the mixed economy of provision; the extended boundaries of public management, the relationships involved and how these are best managed; and some aspects of service design. Chapter 9 stands back and tries to tease out the people implications of what has been discussed in terms of experience, skills needed and personal development. In each chapter the key points of the agenda are highlighted.

USING THE BOOK

The agenda, in whole or in part, can be used by the reader individually, or by a group or organisation as a starting point for reviewing the current state of affairs and exploring the kind of changes which might be considered or initiatives taken. While it in no sense pretends to be exhaustive it is a starting point and focuses on key issues which will be familiar to most readers. The book is the result of having watched and worked with many local authorities and outside organisations involved in local governance. The issues are the ones which, time and again, have been centre stage.

In addition to the highlighted items on the agenda, each chapter concludes with questions which can be used — again individually or collectively — to review progress and to think how things might be difficult. They will be useful as a way of forcing thinking and discussion. Questions demand answers!

The book is designed to be dipped into and to provoke. Precisely because it will raise more issues and questions than suggest answers or solutions, there are, at the end of the book, some suggestions for further reading.

The actual way in which the book is used is over to you, the reader . . .

2

The agenda

<u>KEY POINTS</u>

- Changing local government and the new local governance.

- Politics and leadership.

- Purpose and direction.

- Organisation matters.

- Closer to the people.

- Commissioning and services.

- People.

This chapter sets out the agenda which is identified as this book unfolds. Taken together it provides the basis for reflection review — and action — at a personal or organisational level. Its sections relate to the book's chapters.

❏ Changing local government and the new local governance

- *The importance of mapping external change and testing out its implications. To do this requires standing back from the past, both in terms of trying to construct as full a picture as possible and in not being trapped by personal and organisational experience and expectations.*

This is more difficult than it looks. There is a complex backcloth of change in society at large (social, economic, demographic, technological, etc.) and a domestic agenda within local government — much of it prompted by central government policy and legislation — as well as change prompted by local choice and local circumstances. It is imperative to stand as far outside this as possible and try to discern what the key strands are and where it might be leading. This requires time, effort and space. Without it it is difficult to begin to chart any kind of course.

- *Think local governance and look for ways of both making explicit and strengthening the process which brings organisations and agencies together into the shaping of the locality and its public provision, and defining the local authority's role within these processes.*

Local governance involves not just the local authority but a whole range of organisations and agencies in the public, voluntary and private sectors. Together they play a part in shaping direction and making public provision for the locality. Local government is in the process of re-discovering its role in community leadership. This has been partly the result of a greater fragmentation in local governance and of a recognition of the many agencies and organisations involved. Thinking local governance rather than just — institutional — local government is important. For the good of the local community it is important to find ways of trying to build processes which give the explicit form and enable collaborative and co-operative effort where this is appropriate. The local authority comes into this as a multi-functional organisation and, above all, with its democratic legitimacy. It thus has a key role to play. But what? There is no blueprint and its leadership is certainly not guaranteed. Imaginative thinking and effort are needed. The various actors could be left just to get on and 'do their own thing' — and this will be right for much of the time — but issues transcend organisations and boundaries, synergy comes from joint action and resources will be better used if there are shared understandings about priorities and needs.

- *Local public management needs to be re-defined and an effort made to identify and articulate shared values, styles and approach.*

There are important distinctive characteristics of management of local government as such, just as there are things which are distinct about managing in the public domain generally, as opposed to managing in the private or voluntary sectors. It is important to be clear about the distinctions and to know what is special about local government — or whatever — and what its implications are.

However, there are dangers in pursuing the logic of these distinctions too far. In reality, boundaries are blurred and becoming more so. The mixed economy of service provision, the collaborative partnerships in, say, re-generation or community development, the concern for the 'health' of the local community, bring different organisations and sectors together more than separating them. Local governance is about spanning and managing boundaries. Of course there will be distinct agendas, values, and interests, but there will also be things in common.

In this new situation, putting a narrow exclusive boundary round local, public management is not helpful. A different perspective is needed. There is need to search for the common values and principles and the ground which can be shared in terms of style and approach and to look for ways in which these can be strengthened — albeit in the context of each organisation's more limited, domestic agendas and motivations.

- *Public management needs to be thought about in terms of constant transformation and renewal.*

This is a simple, but important point. The language of 're-invention' and 'management revolution' has become commonplace. This may be helpful in underlining the need for major change, but it implies a once and for all discontinuity. The importance of the continuing search for improvement; the learning which is an essential ingredient of government and governance; the constantly changing environment within which it happens; and the need for all those involved to be exploring new ideas and approaches is caught better by an emphasis on evolution and transformation. It is to this end that this book's agenda is directed — notwithstanding the fact that challenges for local public management are greater than ever before.

❑ Politics and leadership

Every council needs to

- think through and define member roles and ensure that political structures and processes are in place to support them;
- make a conscious effort to develop trust and good working relationships across the officer–member divide, with shared understandings about respective roles and relationships;
- ensure elected members have adequate levels of research and officer support, together with access to training and development to help improve individual capacity and performance.

11

That is a formidable agenda in its own right. Underlying it are some straightforward, and fundamental, points. Despite all the rhetoric and a succession of attempts to generate debate and action over the years, there has been less change in political management arrangements than might be expected by the extent of other changes. In many councils, roles are diffuse and not thought through; consequently the matching of structures and processes to what has to be — or ought to be — done is more by luck than anything else. If elected members are going to 'steer', shape direction, make choices and decide priorities and then review and evaluate, they have to have the mechanisms and instruments to do it. Much of what actually goes on does not help these roles, let alone the role of representation.

For elected members to have the confidence to tackle their jobs properly, play a full part inside the authority and in the wider arena of local governance, and to work competently with officers, they must have access to good research and office support and the opportunity to develop knowledge and skills through dedicated training development.

- *Political parties and party groups should review their ways of working to ensure openness and integrity in political management, and that they do not inhibit its capacity to be outward looking and responsive.*

Political parties dominate the political management of most local authorities. They have an enormous impact but there is little discussion of the way they work. Too often there seem to be signs of exclusiveness not inclusiveness, closed discussion not open discussion, decisions taken with inadequate debate and information and on the basis of narrow interest rather than careful weighing of competing interests, and of unnecessarily strong group discipline. Such things do not square with an increasingly plural and diverse society.

Politics is an essential ingredient of local government: there are competing values and interests and limited capacity and resources. Difficult decisions and judgements have to be made. Not only should party political activity be based on high standards of conduct, it should be kept under regular review and debate by all concerned. Such debate needs to be as open as possible — if it is not, it only serves to create further suspicion.

- *Local political leaders need to recognise other sources of local leadership, develop collaboration with them and, also, find ways of drawing them into their own processes.*

However important and distinct the council's political leadership, there are other sources of leadership in the locality. These groups have an important part to play in local governance. Political leadership needs to recognise and find ways of working with other leaders to develop a collective and collaborative capacity. To do this successfully, opportunities must be found to draw others into the internal processes of the local authority. Equally important, the political leadership needs to think how the local authority, with its wide range of resources and functions and its legitimacy, can best exercise overall leadership and how it can both establish and develop such a role.

- *Attention needs to be given to the local democratic deficit in local governance.*

The local authority draws strength from its democratic roots — even though we shall argue later that they need strengthening. The wider arena of local governance lacks a local democratic base. Ways need to be explored of using the local authority to fill some of this gap, of taking steps to encourage as much openness as possible in debate, discussion and decision-making to ensure public confidence and ownership in what happens and of developing mechanisms for improved local accountability. The council itself can play a part in opening other agencies to scrutiny and review but it will need to recognise the dilemma of being both a potential critic and wanting to be a partner and collaborator at the same time.

- *Structures and processes are necessary to give form — and legitimacy — to what is happening in local governance.*

It is easy to imagine that co-operation in local governance will just happen and that organisations and leaderships will simply come together and make it all happen. Where there is a will things will happen, but structures and processes are needed to cope with the continuing relationships. They provide a framework which is understandable from the outside, provide legitimacy, and bring the pressure to deliver which comes from formality and openness. Structures and/or processes should not be allowed to grow into another piece of bureaucracy; all they need to be is sufficient to make things happen.

- *Ways need to be found to strengthen local representative democracy and also to share power in decision-making and in the management of services and local institutions.*

Local representative democracy may not be as strong as sometimes assumed. A great deal of weight is placed on the councillor as representative and thus on the power of the ballot box. There is a need to find ways of strengthening representative processes; both through the representative role of the

13

councillor and by using devices which inform decision processes by exposing the views and judgements of citizens — citizens' juries, focus groups, user panels and so on. There is also good reason to find ways of allowing citizens to participate more fully, whether in making decisions or taking part in the direct management of services or local service institutions. The result is both strengthening representative democracy and encouraging participative democracy, and helping to re-connect citizens to *their* local government and increasing a sense of local identity and ownership of what is going on.

❏ Strategy and purpose

- *Leaders — members and officers — need to define a sense of purpose for the organisation and to identify key values for it.*

Any organisation needs a sense of purpose and direction if it is to make the best use of its energy and resources. Shared values emerge which then galvanise the commitment and motivation of staff. Local government is more complicated than most organisations because of the respective roles of elected members and officers. The local authority has a political direction as well as an organisational purpose. Its purpose and values will also have a wider role than in many organisations: they must engage the interest of citizens as well as employers.

It is too easy to assume that aspirations and sentiments are shared. Special effort must be taken both in defining them (ideally involving people right through the organisation when formulating the definition) and in making sure that they stick. Values and a sense of direction which do not 'belong' to everyone are unlikely to have much impact.

- *Strategic management is important. Organisations need to be aware of those changes which will cause them to act differently, to prepare for and manage them and to carry through the changes required.*

We have already identified the need to understand the changes happening. Some of them will be coped with in the ordinary course of working; others will demand new approaches and ways of working. Being able to identify the latter, choose where to concentrate efforts and then to ensure that the changes are seen through, is what strategic management is all about. It is too easy to become so all-consumed with managing day-to-day operations and 'incremental' change so that the discontinuities and the big issues are lost sight of. The key tasks of strategic management are about protecting space so this does not happen and developing the capacity to deliver whatever changes are involved.

- *Ways should be sought to develop a strategic approach to local governance; this is likely to include establishing a forum where an understanding can be developed about what is happening to the locality, choice can be made and priorities selected and which has a capacity to oversee and monitor change.*

A locality, like an organisation, needs a 'strategic sense', some kind of purpose or direction which can shape the contribution of its various constituent parts. The point has already been made that structure and process need to underpin local governance. These can be used to develop shared understandings and to resolve conflicting interests and values. Unlike strategic management in any single organisation there is no one person or group who can ensure delivery and who has any sanction over the organisations involved. Voluntary involvement and self-regulation are the keys to success. However it is managed, the objective is to develop a widely shared sense of direction and/or purpose and to make sure that, as far as possible, the organisations and agencies involved are all 'singing off the same hymn sheet'.

- *A strategic planning and research and intelligence capacity is necessary.*

For all the scepticism about planning, an attempt to take a longer term perspective on key issues and activities is important – notwithstanding the high levels of uncertainty in which local government is operating. It needs to be fed by a research and intelligence activity which provides the information to challenge assumptions, leads the search for new ideas and approaches, and is able to think outside established patterns and conventions. This capacity can be organised in a number of different ways. Substantial parts may be capable of being bought in or developed collaboratively with other partners in local governance.

- *The lateral or horizontal connections between areas of policy or action are important. Many issues do not fit into established boundaries. Problems and issues need to be seen as wholes.*

There are too many examples of organisational boundaries (internal or external) getting in the way of issues, problems and opportunities which, to be tackled successfully, demand 'boundary spanning'. The capacity and inclination to see 'wholes' and to act laterally is essential, as are the organisational approaches which encourage rather than inhibit. However strong the pressures to act independently — and they are strong — they must be resisted. Structures, processes, style and people are needed to make sure there is integration not fragmentation. The issue is important for the local authority itself, with its own internal boundaries; it is also critical in local governance and for the boundaries between the multiplicity of organisations which are involved.

■ *A central or strategic 'core' is needed to drive corporate and strategic processes; it needs to include strategic managers from across the organisation.*

An important part of a local authority having a strategic capacity and the ability to see the 'whole' and act on it, is to have a 'centre' which is able to stimulate, support and drive and to ensure that the various structures, processes and people do their stuff. The focus will be the chief executive and political leadership; there will need to be some kind of support staff, however small; senior managers from functional and service areas, who have a strategic responsibility and who thus bring a range of special perspectives into the wider debate and view, need to be involved.

❏ Organisation matters

■ *Organisation must be seen in terms of structures, processes and people.*

It is tempting to talk of organisations only in structural terms. Structures are important, but so are the processes — and systems and procedures — which underpin them and the people who make them work. It is important that the various facets of organisational life are held together as a whole. To concentrate on one without the others is to weaken the whole.

■ *Organisations are important and their design needs to fit the purpose they are there to serve.*

This is another obvious point but another which is easily missed. Organisations evolve and purpose changes. The mismatch between the two can happen without notice or design. Different organisational designs help or hinder the fulfilment of different purposes. Any local authority — or service or function, for that matter — needs to go back to basics and ensure that purpose is being supported by the right kind of organisation. Where it is not, changes need to be made.

- *Any organisation is differentiated in some way; compensatory mechanisms need to be developed to produce integration or fragmentation will result.*

There are many dimensions of differentiation. Different ones will be emphasised in different organisations. Each will encourage limited perspectives and/or partial action. Means of integration need to be developed to prevent fragmentation and the inability to handle the 'whole'. Where there is fragmentation (differentiation without integration) the question of making fundamental changes to deal with it need to be addressed. Traditional patterns of differentiation are typified by service departments and committees; newer ones by the client–contractor split. Some means of integration (i.e. decentralised arrangements which bring services together at the most local level) can themselves be the source of further differentiation or even fragmentation.

- *Local governance is highly differentiated; structures and processes have to be developed to facilitate integration between organisations and agencies.*

The world of local governance, comprising as it does a whole range of separate organisations and agencies (public, private and voluntary), is by its nature differentiated. This does not matter where organisations have straightforward, independent tasks to perform; but where co-operation is needed to deal with particular problems or issues or to advance the general interests of the locality, machinery and processes which integrate are clearly essential. The structures and processes, which we have said are desirable to give form and legitimacy, can thus begin to fulfil a more substantial role. Integration is unlikely to happen without them.

- *Change is continuous and not a periodic happening on the way to a new stability; change needs to be properly prepared for and adequate time allowed for it; its management involves managerial and leadership skills of a high order.*

A period of change is often characterised as an unfortunate necessity on the way to a new stability. This is not an adequate description of most contemporary change. That is better seen as being more or less continuous. People and organisations need to understand this or frustration and cynicism will creep in when stability does not materialise.

The management of change is therefore, a key part of the management task. Evidence suggests it is often something inadequately done. In particular, careful preparation is necessary and realistic time allowed for it to be successful. Much change involves changes in culture, attitudes, skills and working practices. Such things do not happen overnight.

Evidence also suggests poor leadership and too little concern for the people involved. Change management, if it is to be effective, means giving time and careful attention to people issues involved and making sure that, as far as possible, people are carried with it rather than fighting to resist it.

   ■ *When organisations are re-designed jobs need re-designing too;*
     management jobs need particularly careful thought and definition.

'Delayering' and 'downsizing' are fashions of the time. They may well be justified but if organisations are to be re-designed jobs must be treated in the same way — or else fewer people will be doing the same amount of work, often with destructive consequences. Different functions and activities, moreover, will need different intensity of staff support and managerial checks and balances. In re-designing jobs, particular attention needs to be given to managerial roles, their content and the balance between managerial and operational responsibility. Some organisations may find they have too many managers — often the result of the way they have grown rather than any conscious decision. A capacity for innovation and development needs to be built in.

   ■ *In thinking about purpose and getting the organisation right,*
     consideration of learning capacity and the kind of learning which is
     needed is an essential ingredient.

Governmental organisations are about learning — learning from their environment and their operation what needs to be done and how. Organisational arrangements can enhance or inhibit learning. An important part of organisation design is making sure that the learning processes are fed and supported. Defining purpose as the prelude to designing organisation gives an opportunity to ensure that the right value is placed on learning.

❏ Closer to the people

   ■ *Members and officers need to share an understanding of the kind*
     of relationships which are to be built with public and community.

'Top-down' views of what the local authority does and how it should work need to be balanced by 'bottom-up' ones. The extent to which the latter will be forthcoming or successfully formed will depend, in large measure, on the kind of relationship the council builds with the outside world. This relationship needs to be consciously shaped — and an understanding of it shared across the member–officer divide. It thus needs explicit discussion and definition.

- *Decentralisation provides a useful means of being 'closer to the people'; any moves towards it need to be accompanied by clear thinking about objectives and what needs to be done to make it work.*

Decentralisation covers a wide range of possible arrangements — some limited to the inside of the organisation; some managerial and some political. There are good examples of success but there are many of problems and even failure. The latter usually comes from ambiguous objectives and/or raised expectations followed by frustration and resentment. Careful definition of what is involved and to be achieved is essential, just as is consideration of the corporate framework and clarity about what is to be held at the centre and not delegated. Preparation, support, training and the like are also crucial as people will need to act in new ways and the organisation behave differently.

- *Local 'local governance' is also a way of bringing government closer to citizens and communities.*

At the most local level, the business of governance also involves a range of organisations and interests. These can all be left to operate separately, or they can be brought together with the objective of making maximum impact and best use of resources. As with any kind of inter-organisational working there needs to be an open discussion of working relationships and possibilities, recognition of strengths and weaknesses and the development of shared understandings, approaches and agendas. This will almost certainly need some formality and framework to give it lasting presence and clout. In shire areas the role and relationships of country district and parish councils will be an important part of this.

- *Communities of interest are important as well as communities of place; members and officers need to think through urgently new relationships between local government and the rich diversity of voluntary and community interests.*

A hallmark of a plural society is a plurality of interests. Such communities of interest are important for most people — often as important as geographical communities. They engage high levels of personal investment and

19

commitment. Local government needs to recognise them as it instinctively recognises place and to find ways of inter-acting with their organisations. It also needs to develop processes which draw their members and representatives into the council's life and business. Such communities and organisations have important potential for drawing closer to the people and re-connecting citizens to *their* local government.

> ■ *Getting service relationships right is also an important part of being closer to the people and this involves all facets of organisational life.*

One of the most difficult parts of leading and managing any service organisation is maintaining an outward looking 'customer' focus. All kinds of things get in the way and encourage inwardness. Right relationships involve all parts of the organisation: structures, processes, and people (culture, skills and so on). They also require improved techniques for listening and finding out, recognising users as co-producers and educating and supporting users to be more effective. As mixed economies of provision are developed, local authorities are required not just to act for their own organisations but also to try and ensure the same characteristics are shared by all providers.

❏ Commissioning and services

> ■ *The concept of 'commissioning' is important; organisational arrangements need to be in place to support an assessment of local needs, to define priorities and choices, to determine how they are best delivered and to oversee implementation.*

Notions of 'purchaser' or 'client' are too narrow. The concept of 'commissioning' is more helpful and needs to be taken seriously. It involves an emphasis on assessment of need, judgement of priorities and choices and about the best means of delivery, choice of deliverer and oversight of implementation. New kinds of professional skills — going far beyond just managing contracts, the hallmark of the 'purchaser' — are needed and clear roles opened up for the politicians. The idea of commissioning draws the wider locality into the process. The local authority cannot assess needs and determine provision alone; it needs to interact with the community at large in particular, and with its partners in local governance.

> ■ *The decision about appropriate policy tools and instruments and thus the best means of delivering a particular service or activity is a*

key part of the commissioning process. It needs to be approached with an open mind and with no set assumptions. The full range of possibilities needs to be considered and the best alternatives carefully weighed.

In the past it has been easy to assume that a task, once decided on, is best done in-house. This assumption has prevented most councils exploring options and thus the use of some important policy tools and instruments. Traditional in-house provision may be best, but the judgement needs to be made with case and against clear citizens; then there is the question of deciding the way in which it is carried out. These questions are key ones for elected members and for managers. The fact that they are asked with increasing frequency is a welcome consequence of changing ideas and attitudes over recent years.

- *Contracting may be useful as a tool, but costs as well as benefits need to be weighed and the kind of contract for any given situation carefully determined; the possibilities for developing long term contractual relationships need to be explored.*

Contracts have become commonplace in local government life. CCT and the like have put the 'classic' contract to the fore (the detailed agreement, lasting some time and with close specification of what is to be provided). Such contracts fit situations of stability and certainty. They are not so good where neither is present. A different kind of contract, more open, less detailed and implying a continuing relationship and reasonable trust, may be more appropriate. Where contracts are appropriate, careful consideration needs to be given to the kind of contract and relationship which is desirable. In particular, the possibilities which arise from the use of 'relational' contracts need to be explored and exploited.

- *However difficult it may be, it is important to radically review organisations and activities to ensure that resources are being used in the best possible way; in particular white collar and professional jobs need to be closely looked at and overheads kept to a minimum.*

There is a tendency for many organisations to be 'thick' rather than 'thin' — for them to grow by accretion and for unnecessary tasks (particularly support activities) to go unchallenged. Given that resources for service delivery are going to continue to be scarce; it is crucial that every effort is made to ensure there is no 'waste'. It is also important that resources are being properly directed towards priorities and that the balance of spending between services and, within services, between areas of activity is an accurate reflection of political decisions. This, again, is often more difficult to achieve than it sounds. Rigorous monitoring and review are needed.

- *Service design needs to ensure that there is no unconscious discrimination or inequity in access or delivery of service and that proper attention is given to generating explicit criteria for rationing and for the definition and assessment of quality and to providing systems for complaints and redress.*

Service design — another important commissioning responsibility — has many facets. Four are singled out for special note.

- *Discrimination* easily creeps into service delivery and needs stringent action if it is to be prevented;

- *Rationing* is a fact of life in most public services — it needs to be recognised and the criteria used carefully defined and openly articulated;

- Criteria and standards are also needed to determine *quality* and to assess it despite all the advances in 'customer care' and the like;

- There is still, too often a lack of user-friendly *complaints and redress procedures.*

Lastly, in developing policy *and* practice there should be a willingness to pilot and experiment. Good management practice should include a willingness to experiment and test new ideas and approaches to ensure that, when change is made, it is as well grounded as possible. Such an approach implies that mistakes may be made and that success and failure will be a source of learning.

❑ People

- *It is helpful to visualise the organisation as a community with members rather than employees.*

There are different ways of looking at organisations: some mechanistic and some organic. The idea of 'community' is helpful in that it emphasises a number of mutual obligations and responsibilities. It also sheds light on the common interests of members and staff — albeit that the former have particular responsibilities for direction — and on the mutuality of the relationship between the two. Each will bring particular skills and experience but the contribution of each needs to be respected by the other.

■ *The new management of local government needs to be quicker to adapt to change and better able to deal with the fast moving world which confronts it.*

This flows from the other parts of this agenda. What it means is that there must be a greater investment in people and in encouraging and rewarding learning and flexibility. The organisation needs to play its part through support and help, and by ensuring that its culture and working practices do not get in the way of either learning or flexibility.

■ *While procedures and processes need to be put into place to facilitate boundary spanning people and their skills will be crucial.*

A repeated theme of the agenda is the need for working across boundaries (internal and external). A range of skills are needed and they are not always ones which are well represented in traditional local authority settings. They need to be developed and rewarded. At the same time staff involved in such work need to understand the nature of the organisation they are dealing with and the way in which they work. They need to understand, too, that goals and objectives will often emerge from the creation of working relationships and not precede them as conventional management theory might suggest.

■ *Career patterns need to change. More conscious and systematic thought needs to be given to ways in which broader experience can be gained. This will involve opportunities inside and outside local government.*

The new requirements of public management will be best served by the development of new career patterns which span functions, services, disciplines and organisational boundaries. These may be short term and temporary (e.g. secondments and attachments) or they may be permanent. They imply the organisation is taking a more active role in exploiting opportunities as well as exercising imagination. New patterns are capable of being created within local authorities, between them, with other agencies involved in community governance and with organisations beyond. They will serve to develop new patterns of management as well as giving a deeper understanding of other organisational settings — and enhancing working between organisations.

- *Management training and development has an important part to play in renewing local public management and must be used accordingly.*

Management training and development has an obvious part to play in developing new skills and styles of management appropriate to the changed situation. It is important, therefore, that its curriculum is attuned to the new needs and not to those of yesterday. It is important that it also provides intellectual stimulus and is directed to an holistic view. After all the management task is greater than the sum of its parts. It can also provide a way of developing understanding and contact across the various organisations involved in local governance — programmes and activities can be developed collaboratively.

- *Organisation development needs to go hand in hand with the development of people.*

The agenda signals a whole range of ways in which local authorities have changed or need to change. Taken together they emphasise the need to take a positive attitude towards developing adaptability. While the key responsibility lies with the chief executive and senior management colleagues, some kind of dedicated resource will be needed in support. The person or people involved need to have appropriate skills plus an understanding of the organisation and its life. Ideally this resource should be part of the personnel/HR function.

- *Elected members should see their own personal and organisational development as important.*

Whatever reservations members may have had in the past about their training and development, there is a growing recognition that they need support as much as officers do. Skills, knowledge and understanding are essential given the increasing complexities of both their task and the issues with which they have to deal. The importance of the structures and processes of political management supporting their changing roles emphasises the need to make sure that these are continually being developed to match their capacity to requirements.

- *Developing a culture of learning is a crucial part of developing the learning organisation. Organisations cannot learn if people do not learn.*

Setting an example about willingness and capacity to learn is an important responsibility for managerial and political leadership. Part of this encouragement must be about recognising the importance for individuals of personal learning, education and training. Part of developing a culture of learning will also be ensuring that, formally and informally, the organisation promotes rather than inhibits a capacity to learn. The barriers and inhibitions — and their opposites — will be readily revealed through an 'audit' of sources and channels of learning, assimilation processes and the way in which response happens.

- *A special effort needs to be made to help those inside local government and involved in the wider local governance explore and understand the nature of public management.*

Those involved with local government need to understand what is distinctive about it and the values and purpose involved in its management and leadership. Important as there distinctions may be, they need to be kept in perspective. Many others in the locality are involved in public management through their association with local governance. Together, all of them need to explore the common ground which draws them together in serving the public and promoting its good. There will be values and imperatives which separate but there will be those which unite.

HOW TO USE THIS CHAPTER

- The agenda can be used together or in parts.

- It can be used by you individually or collectively by members and/or officers.

- It can be a basis for discussion with others involved in local governance.

- Whoever it is used by or with, its purpose is to prompt reflection and review, stimulate ideas and lead to action to continue the renewal of local public management, improve its effectiveness and make for good local governance.

3
Changing local government and the new local governance

KEY POINTS

- The changing environment.

- Change and local government.

- The new local governance.

- Changing public management.

- Continuing transformation and renewal.

❏ The changing environment

Local government does not exist in a vacuum. It has to respond to — as well as help to shape — the environment in which it is set. That environment has been undergoing enormous change. An example makes the point. There are two local authorities, not far away from one another in the middle of England, which capture a lot of what has been going on. One is heavily industrial, its manufacturing base decimated by the recession of the early 1980s and its attempts to re-build and diversify badly upset again a decade later. There is unemployment — pockets of it very high. The large ethnic minority populations are particularly badly affected. Across the whole population there is a lot of part-time working, and an air of economic insecurity. Parts of the town exhibit high crime rates and public safety is high on the local agenda. The figures show evidence of family breakdown; and there is a high proportion of single parent families. There is a major drugs problem in part of the town; and there is a large HIV community. At the same time there are all the outward signs of prosperity and material comfort in many other parts of the town.

Voluntary associations and sports and leisure activities thrive, in sharp contrast to the sense of exclusion and alienation felt often only streets away.

A couple of dozen miles away is a district council area of lightly populated countryside and small towns. Commuters and the wealthy retired give an air of well-heeled tranquillity. House prices are still relatively high. The population is ageing, however, and there is a disproportionately high number of frail elderly. Local youngsters find it difficult to buy into the housing market and so move away. Farming and related rural industry, once dominant, now employ few, whereas tourism and leisure industries with their 'multiplier' effect thrive. There are increasing numbers of 'tele-commuters'. There is passionate advocacy of 'sustainable communities' and furious opposition to development proposals. Car ownership is well above the national average and public transport has more or less withered away. Village shops and post offices are disappearing fast. . . .

The catalogue of description could go on. Both examples will be recognisable. They serve to remind us both of the enormous change taking place in society and its local diversity. The environment within which local government works and local governance takes place is changing fast.

The litany of these changes is increasingly well documented and familiar. Understanding them is a key part of understanding the agenda. Yet, in the middle of them, it is not always easy to discern their significance or direction, particularly when they may conflict with one another. They include the following factors.

Social change

Social attitudes, structures and behaviours are re-shaping. The family unit has weakened, increased numbers of children are born outside marriage and there has been a steady increase in the number of single parent families. Increasing evidence is available about the growing independence of women and their changed role in the economy and the family. More diverse patterns of lifestyle have become acceptable. That is part of an increasing plurality in society which, in turn, is well illustrated by the growing cultural and ethnic diversity of many cities and towns. Leisure interests are changing and the demands on time and its use are shifting. There are growing signs of alienation in parts of society — alienation from conventional mores and behaviour and, more broadly, from social order and the traditional institutions of society. This is at its most obvious among young people with no job or prospect of a job, living in the apparent hopelessness of the inner city or the outer estate, but its roots spread beyond these stark boundaries. 'Social exclusion' is a new term on the public policy agenda, but it points to something real.

27

The strains within society, and the fruits of alienation, are seen in the statistics of crime and vandalism. These may vary geographically but they have created a climate of concern — and often fear. 'Public safety' is well up most people's list of issues to be tackled.

Personal conceptions of place (home, recreation, work) have changed. For many, despite, or perhaps because of, increased mobility, defence of place against development and change (the NIMBY syndrome) has become more marked. Consciousness about personal health and well-being is matched by growing concern for the well-being of the environment — despite the high value placed on car ownership!

Demography

We are an ageing society. The birth rate has fallen to the point where the working population is not replacing itself. Longevity means an increasing number of elderly, retired people — particularly those described as the 'frail' elderly. On these trends an increasing number of people who have retired from work will be supported by a declining number of people in work. In the longer term that raises massive questions about the financial support of the economically inactive. More immediately there are profound issues about changing patterns of demand on local services and the local economy.

Just as social change manifests itself in different ways in different places, so it is impossible to generalise about demographic change. Some communities have younger age profiles than others. There are places, for example, where the school age population is increasing, just as there are places where there is marked deadline. The capital invested in school provision is not readily portable; moreover, the lead time needed for investment in buildings is long. Many local authorities are still scarred by the 'unexpected' falling rolls of the 1980s. The reaction to that has led some not to notice the differential growth of recent years.

The economy

Economic change is even more significant. Some people have argued that, although society has always been in the midst of change, in the past it has been steady and incremental. Now it is of a different order. Steep changes are taking place and real discontinuities appearing. Such arguments are obviously debatable, but a glance at the economy over the last two decades reveals some evidence.

The recession of the early 1980s changed the face of 'manufacturing Britain'; the recession of ten years later pricked the bubble of the financial and service sector. Patterns of employment have changed. Less full-time work; more part-time jobs, with a disproportionate number of women in the latter but a growing number of men. The 'job for life' mentality has been severely dented in much of the economy. The labour market may have become more 'flexible' but insecurity and uncertainty (ably fed by the vagaries of the housing market) have increased. Localised pockets of long term unemployment are a reality. Disparities between those who 'have' and those who 'have not' have increased.

Arguments about the North–South divide and other such generalities about economic activity conceal both harsh realities and economic opportunity. Across the whole of the country prosperity and economic deprivation lie check by jowl. Merseyside and Middlesborough, or the South Wales coalfield and Clydeside ship-building may bear the popular hallmarks of economic decline and communities with high levels of unemployment and poverty. But even there there is regeneration and parts of the local economy which provide well for some.

Right across the economy, advancing technology is having a massive impact on the nature and design of jobs and on employment. This is a reminder that however distinctive the local economy and whatever the performance of the national one, both are dominated by the global economy and by a transnational economic elite. This elite owes little allegiance to any single country, let alone to Newcastle, Leeds or Plymouth, but has the ability to move capital and investment to the Pacific rim or Latin America or central Europe if that is where the return looks best.

Local government has to respond to the economic circumstances of its locality, and work to do what it can to improve them. It will also be touched by the changing shape of employment and work.

Technology

While it is easy to 'hype' the language of technological revolution, there is no doubting the extraordinary advances of recent years. Its economic impact is seen in the re-structuring and simplification of manufacturing and business processes, with all of its consequences for employment patterns and job design. This is paralleled at the personal level by new opportunities for work, leisure and domestic convenience.

But advancing technology is not just something 'out there'. Many organisations — not least in the public sector — are only just beginning to come to terms with the possibilities for the way they work their structures and processes and for relationships with their customer/client/stakeholder worlds. The potential impact for a local authority is not just in terms of its operating processes, but in the way that new possibilities are opened up for different organisational designs for customer and citizen involvement, for transforming the democratic process, and so on. The technology is about the handling and communication of information; information is the source of power and influence; local authorities are the gatekeepers to vital stocks and sources of information. In an information society, that is likely to have a profound impact on role and relationships.

Of course, there are problems too. Most obvious, is the issue of access. Widespread though familiarity and use of IT has become, there are still large segments of the population untouched or unable to take advantage of the potential. Older people, for example, are much less likely to have acquired familiarity and access; and those who are socially excluded are also likely to be technologically excluded.

Globalisation

It is not just that the global economy has come to dictate national and local fortune, global communication has made the world a smaller place. Trite though that may sound, the capacity for ideas and information to be transmitted across continents and cultures has in a real way transformed society.

Television and the other media bring into the home war as it happens in Bosnia, Iraq or central Asia; exposure to the culture and ideas of Chile or China or wherever; the way in which people live and work and think in parts of the world most people would have had little contact with a generation or two ago; the currency of political debate in California, New Zealand or South Africa... and so the list goes on. The point is simply that in all kinds of ways the horizons of people and organisations are widened, opened to all manner of influences and affected by international trends and actions on a scale which would have been unthinkable not all that long ago.

Expectations

Global information and communication inevitably set new expectations, but they are only one of the influences at work. Increased prosperity has opened new possibilities and demands; the impact of technology has taken us past the era of mass production of identical goods and services which we have to take or leave. We now want, and can have, choice which matches products or services to our individual foibles and preferences. The possibilities for individual choice in the ordinary market place — and our increasing interest in quality — are matched by frustration when they are not available.

Public services may not always be in the market place in the same sense but they do not escape the change — and rise — of expectations. People want to see collective needs met; they also want to see their individual needs and aspirations met in a way which treats them as individuals and in a unique way. Whether or not the (public) resources are available is almost irrelevant to the desire for more and better services. The implications are as massive for public services as they have been for private goods and services. 'Mass production', with minimum concern for individual distinctions, informed the basic design of public service.

The role and scale of government

Though not independent of other changes in society, there is debate in many countries about the nature, role and scale of government. The UK is no exception — except for its inclination to think that this is solely rooted in the experience of 'Thatcherism' and so peculiar to itself. The growth of the welfare state and public provision after the economic crises of the 1920s and 1930s and the Second World War was an international phenomenon in the industrial world. Changing economic fortunes, continual rising expectations and demands and the apparent intractability of many social problems (and the seeming failure, country by country, of chosen solutions) called into question the government's role.

Market liberalisation, the privatisation movement, and the perceived importance of competition and the new forms of regulation which are their consequences, both change and question further the nature of government. Internationally, in regimes of left and right, calls to 'roll back' the state and claw back the boundaries of government have been heard loud and clear even if the reality has not been so dramatic. The collapse of the communist regimes of Eastern Europe and Russia and the end of the 'Cold War' have added to uncertainty and a sense of crisis and questioning about the definition of government and its role. Local government has not escaped this questioning and, of course, in Britain it proved a soft target and starting place to make the 'rolling back' rhetoric a reality. Local government has been in the forefront of the desire to control and, if possible, cut back public expenditure; but that is to take us to a more domestic agenda of change.

Management trends and ideas

Local government management does not take place in a world isolated from other forms of management. Whatever its particular hallmarks or distinctions it is influenced by more general thinking, trends and fashions. Indeed, this has been underlined over the last decade and more, with encouragement to look to private sector management for the models of success. Over that period there have been major shifts in emphasis and priority: the focus on core business; out-sourcing; decentralisation; new models for the centre, with the distinction between the 'loose' and the 'tight' customer responsiveness; quality (with the total quality management movement and its variants); the shift from strategic planning to strategic management and the search, now, to re-integrate notions of planning — albeit taking account of uncertainty; ideas about empowerment and the value of people; performance management; and so on. The list goes on, as could the more general catalogue of change, but the point is made. In many different ways, and with widely varied interpretation, these ideas and developments have penetrated local government and influenced thinking about and approaches to management. Sometimes they have been lumped together and called the 'new public management'. That is misleading in that it implies a coherence which is not there. Not only is there diversity: often approaches seem to contradict one another.

❑ Change and local government

The importance of these changes is their impact on local government and the way it defines what it has to do and how it works. Their range and variety is rehearsed here to make clear that the environment within which the local authority operates has changed and is going to go on changing. Just as it would have been hard to predict twenty years ago the shape of the world in the mid 1990s, so we need to recognise that, say ten years on, things will be different again. Much of this change is, of course, out of the control of governments at any level.

Managing in any organisation has to take account of the environment within which it operates. Local government is no exception. Trying to understand what is going on in that broader environment and to discern its implications and impact is part of good management. Obvious though the point is, the first item for an agenda should be **the imperative of mapping external change and testing out its implications. To do this successfully means standing back from the past, to construct a total picture while not being trapped by our own experience and expectations**. In an era of rapid change and even discontinuity, past trends and present patterns may not be a good predictor of future realities, however important history and experience are in understanding how we should act.

For a local government audience these broader external changes are often obscured by the more immediate changes which arise from the policy and legislation of central government or within local government itself. We need to note these as they are another key part of the context which shapes the agenda. Some of them are, of course, responses to or shaped by the external forces. They include the following:

Finance

Three decades of growth in local government spending began to come to an end with the oil crises of the 1970s, the IMF intervention and the first serious efforts to put downward pressure on public spending ('the party is over' said Tony Crosland as Environment Secretary in 1976). Financial growth had been matched by a growth in powers, responsibilities and activities, reflecting itself in staffing levels.

This growth had been paralleled by a culture which was about doing more and spending more, often matched by a view that complex social problems were capable of relatively easy solutions providing there was enough money to spend. Of course there were differences between the parties about the details of this, but there was broad consensus about the fundamentals; and this was a consensus shared across the officer–member divide.

The last two decades have been sharply different. Even if total levels of local government spending have been cut less sharply than many would believe, the thrust of the rhetoric has been about reduction, about doing more with less, about seeking alternative sources of funding (and thus ways of doing things), and about value for money, and the rest of it. In parallel, central government has taken a series of steps to increase its control over levels of spending and significantly reduce fiscal autonomy, as well as reducing the tax base of local government.

Given the nature of the national economy — and the effects of the global economy — there is little reason to believe that total public expenditure will increase significantly in coming years, whatever party is in government. Controls may be released but the issues of how to best use the limited resources available, against a backcloth of increased demands and rising expectations are not going to go away. In short, if public services are to be extended or generally improved, then money will have to come from internal re-distribution and re-allocation or from new sources.

Nature and role

To simplify a complex picture, the era of growth was characterised by a local government which placed a high value on self-sufficiency and discharging its responsibilities with its own people, using its own organisation and resources. It is hard to believe now but the 1970s re-organisation was largely shaped by this assumption and associated conceptions of economies of scale. A broad consensus about the policy agenda, approach and (professionally driven) solutions marched alongside.

All that has changed. In the 1990s we are not as much at ease with arguments about simple or technical solutions to what we now see to be complex social and economic problems even if some would see the market as a general panacea. The impact of a series of measures and ideas aimed at breaking the provider monopoly of the local authority and a producer driven culture has broken the assumption of self-sufficiency. The wider questioning of the role of government has fed this process, as has the rhetoric of customer choice and the compulsory or voluntary removal of bits of service provision from local authority control. If not at a major turning point, we are certainly in the middle of re-defining local government's role.

Markets, competition and contracting

At the heart of the break up of monolithic service monopolies has been the attempt to develop markets for public services, enforce competition and encourage the development of contractual relationships. The changes have been profound. The development of proper markets may have been limited, but attitudes and approaches to management and organisation have been transformed.

The territory is familiar. Making no judgements about the pluses and minuses, the impact has been far-reaching. Internal relationships and structures (support and front-line services, the purchaser–provider split) have changed; even where contracts have been won in-house, the possibility of there being alternatives has opened up; Voluntary Competitive Tendering and out-sourcing have followed; politicians and managers have been forced to specify, and thus think through, what services are required at what standards and levels; there is new emphasis on performance, monitoring, outputs and outcomes. There is no pretending that these changes have been easy nor that they have always been right — let alone internally consistent; but none should under-estimate their far-reaching significance.

A mixed economy of provision

Partly as a result of competition but partly, also, because of other changes (e.g. opting-out provisions; the community care regime with its requirement to purchase from outside the authority) a mixed economy of local public service provision has begun to emerge. While the local authority never was completely dominant, it is now much less so. Other providers — elsewhere in the public sector, the voluntary sector and the private sector — are increasingly part of a complex web of providers. The role of the local authority as purchaser or commissioner (we shall return to this distinction in Chapter 8) has come into prominence. New forms of management have become important, matching the increased number of providers.

Service changes

There is no local government service untouched by specific changes to its responsibilities or the way it is organised. While many of the changes have been driven by things described above, others have not. The external environment itself has driven policy changes and new patterns for delivery. Services, above all, have to respond to changing demands and new problems. The impact of the Children Act on social services and, indeed, education; the introduction of the National Curriculum; the needs of the frail elderly or the unemployed; and the physical planning framework (e.g. the approach to out-of-town shopping or the changing attitudes to road building) are all examples.

Local fragmentation

Increasing fragmentation has crept into the internal workings of local government as a result of many of these changes. This has provided a new set of challenges for the management of the whole. The same process is visible externally. The development of the mixed economy and contracting with outside organisations has increased the number of players in the service delivery world. There is more, however. In education 'opting out' has given us grant maintained (GM) schools and, in housing, increased involvement of housing associations; some services have simply been removed from local control — wholly, such as FE colleges; or, partially, such as the careers service. New bodies have been created to serve single or special purposes — development corporations, task forces, HATs, TECs and so on — operating at least partly on territory which would have once been the local authority's. The requirements of City Challenge and the Single Regeneration Budget have forced the pace of co-operation and cross-sectoral partnership. The search to find new resources outside the RSG and Council Tax have led the same direction.

New management thinking

The impact of external management ideas and developments has already been mentioned. Independent of the changing approach to management dictated by the factors just outlined, other changes have come from importing and developing of new ideas and techniques. Devolved management;

decentralisation; performance management; and new conceptions of the role of the 'centre' are all examples of often independently inspired initiatives which have impacted on the local authority and the way it is managed.

'Wicked issues'

The local authority agenda is increasingly dominated by issues which do not fit conventional organisational boundaries or ways of working. Economic development, re-generation, community development, public safety and the environment and 'green' issues are all examples of important policy issues which do not fit the still service-based departmental organisation of most authorities or the matching committee structure. They are not obviously owned by any one bit of the local authority. More than that, they very often are not the preserve of the local authority solely. To tackle issues like this successfully requires co-operation with or parallel action by other organisations — public, voluntary and private — in the community. Increasingly, too, it is apparent that the needs of individuals and client groups are often only going to be met by action which spans boundaries and/or requires quite different ways of working. The more such issues and challenges are confronted the more clear it becomes that fundamental assumptions about professional, political, departmental, committee, and organisational boundaries are upset and something new needs to replace them.

Written of in such a way, the internal changes can be made to sound matter of fact, well-ordered and even logical. Of course, reality has not been like that. They have not all been carefully thought through or even, for that matter, all anticipated. They have not all pushed or pulled in the same direction. Some have come quickly, others have been long in generation; few have been adequately prepared for. Often there has been a great deal of learning by (and changing from) doing and experience. In the middle of it, it has probably seemed more like a maelstrom than anything else. Local government has, in characteristic fashion, responded; there has been enormous change. Inevitably it has been patchy — often with more of its consequences met on the officer side of the organisation than on the member one. In many respects, however, implications for both sides are still only being worked through.

As will be clear the internal changes have inter-acted in all sorts of ways with the external ones. This makes the situation even more complicated and potentially unstable. At the same time the local authority has had to relate to the people it serves. Perhaps partly because of all that has been happening but, probably, also because of wider forces at work in our society and beyond there are signs of increasing alienation from, frustration with and cynicism about local democracy and government. If the changes outlined have begged or raised unresolved questions, as important as any are those about the relationship of local governments to their citizens and communities and the meaning of citizenship or, put another way, questions about the way in which citizens do or do not identify with and have a sense of ownership of their local political institutions.

❏ The new local governance

Where does all this take us? On the one hand it gives us the context from which the agenda is drawn or which, at least, shapes it. But it does more than this. The impact of the external and internal changes requires change or renewal of management approach and style inside the local authority. So much is clear; but what should also be clear is that this is only part of the story. A previous generation might have been able to conduct a debate about improvement without looking outside. That has now changed. A whole series of things have made external relationships and their management more important. The agenda requires us to think beyond local government to **local governance**.

The mixed economy of provision, the greater differentiation of organisational arrangements within the local public sector, the importance of partnerships — particularly in social and economic re-generation and the growing importance of wicked issues all play their part in emphasising this wider focus. Additionally, as direct service provision has become less all important for most authorities space has been created to think about the governmental role of the local authority — looking beyond its own services to broader issues of local choice and voice, being concerned with the overall health and direction of the community or locality and using its capacity for influence as well as control.

Together, all of this gives new recognition to the fact that the governance of the locality involves many organisations and people. There is nothing novel about this; it always has been so. However, the numbers of players has increased; the local authority's role has been weakened in terms of its direct contribution; the issues and challenges facing any locality have become more complex; the requirement for joint action between agencies have become more pressing; and the processes of governance have become, or seem, much more complex. In a way the increased pluralism and diversity within local society is matched by a growing pluralism in its governance.

In this situation, local government is having to re-think its role, and society determine anew what it wants from local government. The local authority retains a number of distinctive characteristics of its own. It is multi-functional, whereas most other organisations are not; it has a democratic base which gives it particular legitimacy and strength in taking a broad view; it is large-scale (often the largest local employer, for example) and commands a wide range of resources; it has a wide range of statutory powers and it possesses an enormous amount of information and knowledge. For most local authorities services are still important, and political and organisational arrangements are geared to their production and management. At the same time, for most there is a new willingness to define what it is they are there for in a different way.

We are thus in the middle of another kind of change — a product of much of what has been described earlier but distinct and with its own momentum — a change in the way we perceive and organise the government of our communities. In no sense has it been properly thought through in advance or is anyone implementing a carefully engineered programme. For many, most, in the community at large, the change is barely discernable. It is not clear to those, even in the middle of it, precisely where it is leading or, indeed, what other changes (legislative or locally inspired) may be needed along the way. It presents issues about roles and relationships and about local public management.

The local authority is a forum for local choice and for resolving the conflicts inevitably thrown up by a plural society and plural sets of values. However, it has always been only partial in most of its action — limited to the arena of its services. In one sense it remains so limited. Should that be so? What should its competence be? What is its relationship to other agencies? What is its role? Old style notions of control are obviously inappropriate. The new language of civic or community leadership, with the implication of influence is nearer the mark. But what does that actually mean? How is leadership exercised? What are the implications for internal organisation and its management as well as external relationships? How are these underpinned? What structures and processes are necessary?

The questions come easily, the answers are more difficult to find. That is not the point, however. Our agenda requires local government politicians and managers not to think just of their internal, domestic concerns but to **'think local governance' and to search for ways of making explicit and strengthening the processes which bring organisations and agencies together to shape the locality and its public provision and define the local authority's role within them.**

❑ Changing public management

Two other points arise, both of which return us to issues flagged in the introduction and which need to be firmly noted. The first is that any examination of who is involved in the processes of local governance reveals it is not just local government and other 'public' organisations but voluntary and community ones and, indeed, organisations in the private sector. This raises a question about the definition of local **public management**. The British habit of drawing a tight boundary and distinguishing between people who are employed in public organisations and people employed elsewhere looks misleading in circumstances where boundaries are crumbling. Each organisation and sector places its own demands and requirements on management.

There will be differences between managing a widget and a factory and a private hospital, between a supermarket and a financial services company, between a private school and a department store — let alone between the public, private and voluntary sectors. Equally there will be differences between managing a statutorily based regulatory service and the management of a leisure centre or some other quasi-commercial enterprise. These differences are important but won't there also be similarities between managing a 'voluntarily' provided day centre, or a city challenge partnership activity, or a private sector old people's home or, even, a refuse collection service? Again, key questions. But, as we emphasise local governance and work with a mixed economy of service providers, we may not help by restricting the definition. What is peculiar to the public domain per se? What are the values, approaches which need to be shared more widely across all those involved in public service, regardless of who employs them? What dilemmas arise and what are the limitations? How can/should/could the boundaries be pushed wider? If in thinking about a renewal agenda for local government management, we need to think more broadly across the world of local governance we should be **searching to re-define local public management and to identify and articulate shared values as well as style and approach**.

❑ Continuing transformation and renewal

The second point is a more general one. Any attempt to analyse the changes which have and are taking place reveals an extraordinary complexity and messiness. It also reveals a process which is unfolding as it goes. The interaction of different factors and strands of trends, and the business of implementing any single strand, creates a new, and often unforeseen, round of change. In other words change is constant even if it has speeded up in recent years. It is helpful to think of government — at whatever level — and thus public management as a process of learning and evaluation. The language of re-invention and revolution, with an implication of once-and-for-all discontinuity, rapid change and then the possibility of something more stable, is inappropriate. As we made clear in the introduction it is more helpful **to think in terms of a process of constant transformation and renewal**. This puts an emphasis on the business of exploration and learning and of seeking to meet (ever-changing) new circumstances as they unfold.

HOW TO USE THIS CHAPTER

- What are the most important changes which have affected your authority? Looking ahead are there new and different ones on the horizon? What is/will be their impact?

- What does local governance mean for your locality? How far does the council recognise it? Does this need to change? If so, how?

- How would you define local public management? Where would you draw its boundaries? What are its characteristics and shared understandings?

4

Politics and leadership

KEY POINTS

- Political management; roles, relationships and processes.

- Political parties, groups and discipline.

- Political leadership and local governance.

- The democratic deficit in local governance.

- Structures and process for local governance.

- Strengthening local democracy.

One of the things which makes the local authority distinctive is its democratic base. Many of the bodies involved in the governance of any locality are public organisations. All of them have some kind of line of accountability which reaches via politicians to the electorate. For most of the organisations, however, the line is pretty tenuous with, often, a distant link to a Secretary of State and so to Parliament and the electorate. This is far removed from the immediacy of local government with its direct and close involvement of elected politicians in choice and direction, as well as with the organisation and with the public; and with the constant eye of the public fixed on what is happening.

It is this distinctiveness, and the legitimacy which comes from the ballot box which, we have already argued, gives the local authority a special role in the governance of the community. This is further reinforced by a set of requirements underpinning its public accountability which are more robust than for any other organisation (e.g. audit, openness and public access to information, the ombudsman, etc).

The role of elected members in the (political) management of local government is thus very important. There is a need to ensure that its importance in theory is borne out in practice. For this to happen, the effective and well-performing local authority will require to have in place arrangements for political management which are themselves effective in translating the role into reality.

Given the extent of change, whether driven from outside or internally, there is an obvious question about how well political structures and processes have responded to and accommodated new circumstances. The scale of change and the diversity of local government make the answers complex but in many local authorities there is often a sense that:

- the political management arrangements — structures and processes — have not kept up with the other managerial changes;

- that many elected members fear that the organisational and management changes have served only to reduce their power and influence;

- that discussions about change are difficult because there is an immediate tendency to defend the status quo for fear that the unknown will be worse and marginalise still further;

- that there is confusion about roles and relationships.

In some authorities, where changes have been attempted it has taken little account of how councillors behave and gone against the grain of their world. This has not helped. Lurking in the background there are other issues which, if not taboo, are certainly difficult to talk about:

- What is the impact of party politics?

- What role do party groups play?

- How do they operate?

- What about party discipline?

- How good is the party at reflecting and translating the diversity of a plural community into the decision making process?

Asking such questions is not to deny the validity of party politics. Local democracy and local government is about making choices and resolving often conflicting interests and values. The more diverse and plural a society the more important that becomes. That is a political activity. The issues which should concern are ones about how it happens — not whether it should.

There are then, even deeper questions:

- about the relationships of the elected to their electors and citizens;

- about the strength of local democracy and the identity of ordinary people with it;

- about the realities of public accountability;
- about whether we rely too much on the ballot box as the expression of representative democracy;
- about protest and pressure and how it is handled;
- about the potential for involving citizens.

At first glance these may look like questions beyond the scope of a management handbook. In one sense they may be but in another they are not. They may be questions worthy of separate and more extensive discussion but they are also ones which strike right to the heart of what local government is and thus at the way it works and the way it is managed. Looking beyond the narrow confines of the local authority and into the wider world of local governance, they are also important. What do they say about local government's particular role and contribution? How can they be best used to make more explicit or strengthen the processes of local governance? In short, if its democratic roots and its political management are the distinctive contribution which the local authority 'brings to the table' are we making the best of them?

There are then a set of further questions:

- What is the role of an elected political leadership?
- How does it match with other forms of local leadership?
- How does it work and relate?
- Do the internal political management processes of an authority have a contribution to make outside?

These questions are not new but they are given renewed significance by the emphasis on local governance. Like any set of questions, discussion or debate which touches on the roles, relationships or responsibilities of elected members, however, they need one particular note of caution. The debate or discussion must not be officer centred. Of course, it should cross the officer–member divide but elected members must pick up the issues and questions for themselves. Where it involves issues of external roles and relationships it must draw in people from the outside too. Obvious points, perhaps, but ones often honoured in the breach!

❏ Political management: roles, processes, relationships

Ask any group of elected members to define their role and there will probably be as many answers as there are people. Despite the fact that they are in a sense the bedrock on which the edifice of local government is built there is remarkable confusion and lack of clarity about role. This in turn may be one of the reasons why the political structures and processes of local government do not seem to always match the task which has to be undertaken. (Another, of course, is the uncertainty about the balance in the role of local government and the fact that the political side of the machine was designed for, and usually still gives primacy to, the direct delivery of services.)

Roles

Conceptually, there are a number of distinct roles which councillors fulfil. They are concerned with:

- **Representation** — Councillors are first and foremost elected representatives, acting on behalf of their electors and a particular geographical arena. In this role they are there both to look after the interests of that area and those people and to be a link into the local authority, dealing with local and individual needs, problems, complaints and so on.

- **Strategy** — However it is defined any organisation needs a sense of purpose and direction. For the local authority this starts with the members. Setting a direction, ensuring that this is responsive to change in the external environment, ensuring that the organisation is able to deliver and checking progress is crucial.

- **Priorities and resource allocation** — Whatever direction or strategy is set, priorities have to be defined and resources allocated. Demand and expectation will almost certainly outrun the resources available. Resources will need to be carefully directed and used and difficult rationing decisions will be likely to be involved.

- **Policy development** — Strategy will only deal with key issues of direction. Within any area of activity or interest, policy requires development and determination to shape and guide service delivery or other activity; decisions need to be made about how things are best done and by whom; and quality and standards need to be set, whether delivery is in-house or through an agent.

- **Monitoring and review** — It is no good determining priorities, setting policy and defining standards without then ensuring that they are delivered. Tracking and assessing whether and how this happens is vital. It will apply to things which the local authority does directly and things which are done on its behalf.

- **Community leadership** — Election as a councillor defines a wider leadership role. Members find themselves prominent in their community. They will be drawn into other local activities and they will be appointed to represent the local authority on various outside organisations. This provides opportunities to exercise influence. It also offers important potential for the local authority's role in community governance.

- **Politics** — Councillors as members of parties are there as advocates for particular points of view. They will debate, argue and promote their case and seek publicity for it.

These roles derive from the continuing history of local government as an institution. As ideas and thinking about local governance grow so there will be added new possibilities and ways in which the elected members can play their part, strengthening the involvement of local government as such. Roles will thus continue to develop and change — in particular representative and leadership roles are likely to grow in significance and the balance shift to give more attention to wider community concern as well as the local authority's direct responsibilities.

While it is not difficult to describe roles in abstract terms, reality is obviously much more messy. In the hurly-burly of ordinary council life, councillors and officers will find difficulty in sorting-out and supporting the various roles. In order to bring some clarity and understanding — and to make sure that councillors are made as effective as possible — there needs to be explicit discussion and an attempt to define how things should be, council by council. The words used may be different and the patterns which emerge almost certainly will be — that diversity is the essence of local government. What is important is that the discussion happens — and too often it seems not to. It can be helped by using training and development activities and opportunities.

Part of the messiness, of course, is that the roles overlap with one another and may not be of equal interest or appropriateness to all members. It may be further complicated by the fact that the organisation will focus on some, but probably not all, of the roles. Local circumstances, not least the size of the council and its political make-up, will vary, but attention needs to be given to representative role is important but some may be less interested in strategy than in review or external representation; some will be interested in policy development in very specific fields, and so on. In other words, it may be possible to divide up roles as a way of ensuring effective overall performance. It would be naive, though, to believe that many councillors would detach themselves completely from setting strategic direction or policy or priorities! It is more a question of balance. What is important is, again, the explicit discussion and the development of shared understanding.

Processes

Definition and, possibly, differentiation of roles, leads directly to the question of how these are played out and to the development of appropriate processes and structures. History and tradition have given pre-eminence to the committee as the focal point acting on behalf of the (sovereign) council and subject to differentiation by service and department. In turn this gives emphasis to formality of process and to meetings often based on long agendas and designed to make decisions largely about the running of services. Despite all the changes which have taken place, the committee — and the match with service areas — has proved extraordinarily robust! The central question is whether or not it is reliance on a committee system which meets the requirements of the roles to be played.

This immediately raises issues about executive leadership. Where there is clear political direction or control (by majority or in coalition) does the theory and practice of full council and committee fit? Of course there are statutory constraints on the development of an 'executive' or 'cabinet' model of local government with a different kind of role for the council as a 'legislative' assembly. But, as things stand, in many councils there is a covert set of executive arrangements hiding behind the facade of convention. Do we need to think of radical change? There has been remarkably little willingness to openly discuss alternative approaches and arrangements and propose ways forward (viz the response to the 1992 Department of the Environment/Local Authority Association Working Party Report *Unlocking the Potential* with its suggestion, among others, of enabling powers to experiment with executive models).

Less radically, there are the issues about what other processes and structures need to be developed either to enhance the committee system or to use it in a different way in order that elected members can be more effective. Here there has been more willingness to think imaginatively. Many authorities have taken pragmatic steps to make improvements — though few have taken a comprehensive look at how things might be done better. The steps which have been taken exemplify what can be done, including:

- using the full council less as a formal reporting/decision-making body (important though this may be) and more as a forum for major debate about the affairs of both the council and the locality;

- re-defining committee boundaries and responsibilities to fit better with what the local authority sees as its principal interests and activities;

- being clearer about the role of a policy committee and its relationship to other committees;

- ensuring that agendas are pruned to ensure that members can have the time to concentrate on what is important;

- differentiating agendas and cycles to distinguish between matters for discussion and information, and between strategy, policy development, resource allocation, monitoring and review and external relationships;

- developing less formal mechanisms — panels, working parties and so on — to undertake particular sets of tasks (the formality of committee, for example, may not lend itself to the kind of discussion or development of strategic direction or policy, let alone to scrutiny, monitoring and reviews);

- being explicit about the way in which committees and their supporting structures and processes actually relate to the various aspects of member roles (an examination of committee agendas, for example, leaves questions about how far members ever get into the development of policy or what kind of scrutiny and review ever really takes place);

- using co-option or occasional invitation to draw other organisations, agencies and interests into debate and discussion;

- involving service users and citizens at large in the process of scrutiny and review;

- using seminars and away-days to inform, explore and, above all, to develop shared understanding of issues, problems and opportunities — and of dilemmas, conflicts and differences of view;

- providing support and briefing for external representative duties and building in ways of reporting back — both to help members and to shape the council's influence;

- creating local forums which make the connection between council-wide issues and concerns and the needs, views and aspirations of local neighbourhoods;

- developing mechanisms to ensure that local members know all that is happening in their area and can feed into its shaping and development;

- adequate research and office support to help members in the various elements of their role.

The list can probably be extended but the key point remains the same. The important thing is to develop political structures and processes which match the roles elected members have to perform to ensure that these can be performed effectively and to support them through the organisation and its management structures and processes. The fact that things are often left to chance and haphazard adaptation is an indictment of local government in general and elected members in particular. It is a source of frustration on the inside of local government as well as on the outside for those who have to deal with local government. It also leads to spurious debates about other things, for example that the number of members needs to be dramatically reduced in order to get effective working. If numbers are a problem it is probably only because where there are more councillors there is greater confusion about what to do!

None of that is to imply that the questions about who should do what and how are easy to face or answer. They will challenge traditional conceptions and familiar ways of working. They will also raise questions about motives — and fears either that change may shift (more) power to the officers or (further) weaken the backbenchers as opposed to the frontbenchers. The great irony, of course, is that the member role may have been weakened or backbenchers feel marginalised precisely because the structures and processes of political management are out of tune with what they are supposed to do. Job satisfaction for all councillors, including backbenchers in particular, and a proper definition of roles and relationships between members and officers will be greatly enhanced by getting working arrangements right. To avoid addressing the issues is to store up trouble for the future.

Relationships

The last point reminds us that a vital part of effective local government is the relationship between officers and members. Precisely because local government is rich in its variety and diversity, so the pattern of relationships crosses a broad spectrum. There are lots of examples of good relationships but, regrettably, there are plenty of examples of bad ones. The position is complicated by changes of political fortune, the turnover — and inevitably transient nature — of members, and the way in which local circumstances can change rapidly. And, of course, relationships will be different with front-benchers than with backbenchers.

In any organisation or set of relationships trust is a key ingredient to successful working. Without it there will be suspicion, negative behaviour, an unwillingness to be open and other dysfunctional characteristics. Distrust breeds on itself, just as the more trust there is, so it will be self-reinforcing. Trust does not require personal linking but it does imply respect. In the relationship between members and officers, there needs to be a balance between formality (there is a proper distance to be maintained, the one side is accountable to the other) and informality (sufficient to allow open exchange, frankness and ground to explore and develop mutual understanding if not always agreement).

There is obviously no single recipe for success. Trusting relationships, however important they are and however much easier they make things, do not just happen. They need to be worked at; trust needs to be built. Sometimes this will come easily; sometimes it will be very difficult and require hard work on both sides. It will be at its most important at senior levels in the organisation, with chief executive, chief officers and senior operational managers. It will not happen if there are cavalier, arrogant or dismissive attitudes on either side. Officers can be guilty of writing-off members as an irritant or not up to the job, members of regarding officers as self-seeking and inflexible. Neither attitude will do.

Good working relationships also require an understanding of respective roles, of overall direction and what is to be achieved, and a mutuality which allows scope to exchange and to support what the 'other side' has to do. To pretend that the development of strategy, policy and priorities and so on can be the sole preserve of the elected members is to deny the crucial contribution of experience, specialist expertise and information which officers can bring. Equally, to imagine that elected members should have no interest in implementation, except for scrutiny and review, is to exclude, for example, an important source of understanding about how things happen out there in the community and of learning about what is actually going on and of their role as representative.

Relationships are thus inevitably complex. Again, there needs to be some explicit understanding and even agreeing of conventions or protocols about the essentials. It means talking about them, how they are and how they should be. This demands time and space. There are good examples of councils where relationships were bad and lacked trust but where there has been transformation, having created the time and space to do something about it. This may require some limited external help or facilitation. (A good example is of the large local authority where there was a high level of mistrust and destructive relationships, suspicion that the agenda and interests of councillors and officers were not just different but opposed to what members wanted. Two days away of joint discussion revealed a different situation and a remarkable overlap in what each side thought important and how problems might be tackled. From that point relationships began to transform.)

In the past, officers have often been guilty of cramming agendas with detail, crowding out serious policy debate or presenting policy choices in a way which conditioned the outcome. Members, similarly, are often culpable in their eagerness to become involved in managerial and operational detail in inappropriate ways and in losing sight of the big issues. Getting the balance right is not easy — but it will be greatly helped if there is clarity about roles and relationships and there are structures and process properly supporting them.

Putting all this together, **each council needs**:

- **to think through and define member roles and ensure that political structures and processes are in place to support them, in turn supported by the wider organisation;**

- **to make a conscious effort to develop trust and good working relationships across the officer-member divide, with shared understanding about these roles and relationships;**

- **to make available research and office support must be available, along with access to training and development to help improve individual capacity and performance.**

❑ Political parties, groups and discipline

Political parties have become an accepted part of the local government landscape. The point has already been made that their presence is a corollary of the fact that there is no escaping the choices which have to be made between competing — and often conflicting — values, demands, interests and expectations. The presence of parties thus brings some order to the process and provides for a mediating influence between the various interests. That is all well and good but there are some dilemmas which result and some gaps between theory and practice. This suggests that, again, there are issues which at the very least need exposure, reflection and debate — even if subsequent action is difficult. The problem is that such discussion is often taboo, perhaps because powerful vested interests and a private world are involved. The issues include the following.

The nationalisation of local government

For the most part, local parties are the local manifestations of the national parties; because of this, policy debate, election campaigns and so on are too easily nationalised. National leaderships invest in local control and local elections quickly become referenda on national political performances. This must have implications for the way local affairs are both handled by councils and judged by electors. 'Localness' is constrained though not removed.

The representiveness of parties

We have a small number of parties yet they operate in an increasingly diverse and plural society. There must be a question about their capacity to translate that plurality of interests into manifestos and programmes. As mass membership organisations they have declined in support (notwithstanding the recent increase in Labour Party membership). If they are the machinery for mediation between society at large and the decision-making process, have they the capacity, structures and processes to ensure that the task is effectively carried out? Or are reforms needed?

The exclusiveness of parties

One aspect of this is the temptation to exclusiveness. At one level, parties have to be inclusive in order to invite support at the ballot box, but, at another level, this inclusiveness is not properly reflected in the way they work internally, develop policy, take decisions and so on. How important are particular vested interests? How much effort is made to engage with the plethora of community and voluntary organisations which present important interests and values and where membership is often increasing?

The abuse of election

Though not just to do with parties, there is a tendency for some to believe that success at the ballot box endows the councillor with special powers — that he or she (as well as the party and the group) instinctively know best, know precisely what is good for people and how things should be done. Such views reinforce the potential for partial views and for insulation from the real world of the locality.

Parties as gatekeepers to council membership

Like it or not party machines are key gatekeepers to council membership. Because of electoral boundaries and the vagaries of the electoral system, adoption as a candidate can often be more significant than the election itself. If a local party is more exclusive than inclusive and not particularly representative of the locality, it may well have difficulty in attracting good candidates.

Party machinery and party groups

While it does not necessarily follow, there must be a danger that the local party machine and, indeed, the party group on the council, will be inward looking, the preserve of the enthusiast and arrogant in its exercise of power. Of course, many local parties and groups are far removed from this, but how many regularly challenge and review their operations, their perspectives, their external links and relationships and so on? In many councils group meetings are more significant than committee or council meetings. Images of smoke-filled rooms, private deals, decisions guided by private bargaining or unquestioned idealogy and without adequate information and advice or the benefit of public debate do not enhance people's perceptions of local government. Party groups should be innovative in the way they discuss and work.

Party discipline and the whip

Group decisions are often enforced by rigorous discipline and use of the party whip. The question is whether they are too rigorous and too extensively used? Is adequate distinction made between key policy decisions and other matters? Is there room for the influence of debate — outside and inside the council? What about the judgement individual councillors have to make between local interests and the preferences of their party colleagues — is this properly allowed for? Of course, often there will be a clear 'yes' to these questions. But sometimes there patently is not.

The lessons of balanced councils

The last decade has seen an increased number of occasions where there is no overall party control. Sometimes there has been mayhem or an inability to do much at all. Often, though, there has been accommodation and even transformation. Openness, a willingness to debate and listen, coalition building, new relationships between and within party groups and new links with the outside world have become the order of the day. There are useful lessons about how things can be different.

Constraints of the electoral system and party conflict

The experience of hung or balanced councils points to another dilemma. Good management demands openness in the development of policy and ideas and the ability to take a longer term view. Sharply conflictual politics, the 'winner takes all' effect of the first past the post system and the pressures of the electoral cycle. All encourage partial policy debate (and the tendency to exclude) and shorter term perspectives. Hung councils demand a different approach and show alternative ways of operating.

The ultimate accountability

It is easy to dismiss all or most of the sorts of questions and issues raised, by simple references to the accountability of the ballot box. Individuals and groups are ultimately tested at election time and that is what matters. Reality is not quite so simple; sometimes there is a real conflict, often there is not. The nationalisation of local elections and the vagaries of the first past the post system and electoral boundaries get in the way. Many members and not a few ruling groups are effectively unchangeable in normal circumstances. The argument is thus deceptive and dangerously comfortable. Reality suggests the need to underpin this ultimate accountability with relationships and working arrangements which ensure outwardness, inclusiveness, responsiveness and sensitivity to the diverse values and interests of the local society they serve.

There is no escaping the different judgements and decisions which local politicians have to make and the dilemmas which are involved. It is neither surprising nor reprehensible that political parties have emerged as mediating forces. What is important, for the agenda of political management and, more important, the health of democratic local government is that **political parties and party groups should review their ways of working to ensure that they are bringing openness and integrity into political management and not inhibiting its capacity to be outward looking and responsive.** This means recognising and being able to reconcile the rich diversity and the plurality of local society, building ways of embracing it rather than trying to 'filter it out' with over simplistic approaches and modes of action.

❏ Political leadership and local governance

So far we have only touched on the internal workings of local government. With the wider issues of local governance becoming more important, the question is how it relates to the elected political leaderships and the political management of the local authority. The democratic base of local government,

53

its role and its multiple functions all give it a special position and claim to some form of leadership. But, as is abundantly clear, there are often other powerful players, and other potential leaders. In addition, the past performance of the local authority, perhaps in terms of the dominance of its own services, perhaps because of its inwardness of perspective or its arrogance, or perhaps because it has simply done little or nothing may undermine present action or intention. In short, there is no automatic right of entry to leadership: whatever role the local authority wants to play has to be earned — even if it can bring substantial experience and resources to the enterprise.

The point is well made by a north country authority which identified social and economic regeneration as key issues and recognised that successful resolution could only come through the combined action of all those involved in the governance of the locality. In its own admission, it had been a narrow, closed and inward-looking council dominated by a political group interested in a narrow agenda; it set about transformation. Over a period of years painstaking effort was made to construct partnerships and close working relationships with the private sector, voluntary and community organisations and other parts of the public sector. A common agenda and what is best described as a shared 'vision' was developed and a whole variety of means chosen to implement them.

It is clear in this the council played a central role but, again, in their own admission leadership was shared. The council both 'let go' and brought others into its own deliberations and processes. There is still plenty to be done but what is striking about the example is the way in which perceptions of local council have changed and the way in which it is accepted as having a whole series of resources (functions, powers, money, people, willingness and legitimacy) which nobody else can match and which are now seen to be shared.

The example is not peculiar and time and time again experience seems to offer the same clues for success which involve:

- being clear of the value of working with the wider systems of governance;

- developing an agenda which is widely supported and understood;

- working painstakingly to ensure that there is seen to be openness and a willingness to share;

- understanding and using the resources which lie within the authority to facilitate, support, encourage and stimulate as well as actually to do;

- finding ways of making links between political processes of the council and the wider arena involving:

  — drawing in outsiders

  — using council and committee as a focus for more open debate

  — using them to endorse external debate

  — encouraging the involvement of elected members in the workings of other agendas and organisations.

The danger is that such things seem soft and woolly. There are, of course, hard realities. First, there is no reason why the agenda of local governance should not be as focused and hard-edged as the agenda of the local authority. Second, there are issues to do with power. On the one hand, there has to be a recognition that the local authority has only limited power and that there will be many things which are desirable for the local community but in which others are powerful. On the other, there can be recognition of the need to share power in order to achieve. Thirdly, there is the related question of leadership.

We have said that the local authority is in a strong position to offer leadership. As authorities think through their role in local governance, leadership appears on most of their lists. We have also observed that leadership has to be earned and that 'leaderships' must not be confused with 'control'. But, of course, reality is complicated. Any community has all manner of different leadership groups. Some people because of role or personality will be well known across a whole locality, others will exercise leadership in relation to a particular community of interest (business, trade unions, ethnic groups, special interest groups, churches, voluntary organisations and so on). In other words, just as local society is characterised by its pluralism so local leadership will be plural.

Local political leaders need to recognise this and seek to find and build ways of interacting with those other clusters of community interest. This may be difficult. The splendour of the town hall, the sheer scale of council activity — and the ballot box — easily build insulation and separation. 'It is like having strangers sitting in your own front room' said one political leader about a forum of leaders from various parts of community life drawn together to shape a common agenda for re-generation. Yet if the local authority is to act as leader and the cornerstone of local governance, sharing power and working with other leadership groups are pre-requisites. And, of course, ways also need to be found of involving the general body of councillors in ways which utilise their potential and give them satisfying roles.

To repeat, the local authority *is* different and local democracy *is* important, but there are other avenues of representation and other sources of legitimacy of local leadership. This means that **local politicians have to recognise that they have no monopoly of local leadership, they need to work to develop their capacity (using the authority's resources accordingly) at the same time drawing others into the process.** Underlying all of this is, of course, a definition of leadership which is more about influencing than control, and about a capacity to help transform rather than secure change by edict or unilateral intervention.

❏ The democratic deficit in local governance

We return to the fact of local government's democratic base and the foundation of local accountability which this provides. This, of course, contrasts sharply with other organisations involved in the processes of local governance. Though each will have some accountability to members, subscribers, stakeholders or, in the case of public organisations, to a Secretary of State and ultimately to Parliament, none is directly to the entire locality and most are limited in nature and substance. This implies a democratic deficit in local governance.

Some will want to argue that the best way of dealing with this is to transfer powers and responsibilities into the local authority, strengthening it, and reducing the number of players, so providing for a more ordered local accountability. The chances of this happening are negligible, and, anyway, the very suggestion needs to be challenged given that one of the strengths of a plural local governance is its reflection of a plural local society. The dilemmas are real: local government yearns to be strong, there is a desire for less messiness in local government of any locality and there is a wish to broaden local democracy. Monolithic command structures are a thing of the past, however, and experience tells us that large, unwieldy bureaucracies do not have a good record of responsiveness and flexibility.

A more realistic and sensible way forward is to think what can be done **to build on the various sources of local leadership, to enhance the democratic content and impact of local governance and to strengthen the local public accountability of the various organisations and agencies involved.** Possibilities include:

- Establishing a public forum which brings together as wide a range of community leaders as possible, including the political leadership of the local authority.

- The wider involvement of outside organisations and their representatives in local authority political processes.

- The use of the full council to debate major local issues — with contributions from others involved.

- Public meetings, discussion and debate between agencies and organisations involved in particular issues or aspects of local governance.

- Local agreement on processes and procedures which enhance accountability and their adoption by all involved.

- Development by the local authority, preferably in partnership with the other organisations concerned, of arrangements which scrutinise and review the activities of public providers and the product of joint action and initiative in the locality.

- Use of the local media to expose issues, inform and question.

In all of this the local authority, specifically, will need to recognise a major dilemma. It may well want to use its authority and democratic legitimacy to question, scrutinise and review the action of others and to encourage openness in debate and questioning. In this it will easily find itself criticising and being at odds with — or, at the very least, an irritant to — the very agencies and organisations it will want or need to work with co-operatively in dealing with community problems and opportunities.

There is no escaping this dilemma but elected members and officers will need to recognise it. The best way of dealing with it is to confront it directly, explain it and persuade others that there is more to be gained than lost. 'Quango watching' has become a common practice for many authorities. There are some good examples of thorough scrutiny and review processes, based on willing co-operation, and going on alongside joint action and collaboration involving the same organisations. Here there is an acceptance that constructive criticism need not undermine partnership; and that scrutiny and review will produce support as well as disapprobation.

❏ The need for structures and processes

There is an implicit message in what has been said which needs to be made explicit. If local political leaders are to interact with other leaderships groups, organisations and agencies join together in collaborative working, shared understandings to be gained about a vision or direction for the locality and key issues identified, action taken, and so on, then some kind of form needs to be given to that process. This is not to suggest that there is a single approach or that the same models will be portable from place to place.

Inter-organisational relationships are potentially even more complex than intra-organisational ones. They are similar in that they need conscious effort to build them, trust needs to be gained and there needs to be understanding of each other's positions, priorities and ways of working. These things do not just happen; they need to be worked at. The evidence suggests that for this to happen they need **to be underpinned by appropriate structures and processes which support and give legitimacy to what is happening, as well as set the pace and keep track of progress.**

This is not an argument for new bureaucracies. Arrangements can be 'lean and mean'. It is, rather, a recognition that without a degree of formality the best intentions wither. It can also be a way of engineering visibility for a particular set of initiatives or activities and a way of building in a mechanism of accountability. Where individual organisations are making their own separate and distinct contribution to local governance, that is one thing. The thrust of what has been said, however, is that there is increasing pressure and need for inter-action and collaboration in dealing with many issues and aspects of local life. It is for this that the underpinning is necessary.

There are many examples in places up and down the country: partnership organisations (usually in the economic regeneration field); the City Challenge boards; the London, Birmingham and Manchester City Pride initiatives with their formal process to develop vision and strategy; forums bringing together organisations and agencies dealing with a particular client group (e.g. the elderly, young people) or aspect of local life (e.g. environment, tourism, town centre and development, traffic and transport, community development, etc.). In any locality there may be many different arrangements. That does not matter; though, as we shall see in the next chapter, there is a sense of some over-arching arrangement which is able to set strategy and direction and, perhaps, provide some co-ordination.

❑ Postscript : strengthening local democracy

We return to where the chapter started. We have said that local democracy is important. It is the foundation stone of local government. It can also make a vital contribution to the wider process of local governance. Yet it shows signs of being weaker than many would wish: more limited than it seems at first sight. There are important issues to be addressed about how it might be strengthened and its contribution enhanced. The issues are partly national ones — certainly if they involve any change to legislation or regulation. But they are also local ones and need probing and discussing at local level.

Local government places almost total reliance on representative democracy and that, in turn, is heavily dependent on the ballot box. Annual local elections — leaving aside their 'nationalisation' — do not excite. Turnout is seldom more than 50 per cent, often less than 40 per cent. The councillors once elected, though they will, individually, hold their surgeries and be available to their constituents, often working tirelessly to sort out problems, pursue grievances and so on, collectively do little to create processes which support and/or strengthen representative democracy.

There is a new interest in using devices such as citizens' panels, citizens' juries, focus groups, local referenda and so on to inform the policy and decision processes by bringing others in and encouraging debate and exploration of issues and ideas. To pretend that this interest is general would be stretching a point. It is highly selective and often officer driven. Sadly, in some places there is, even now, reluctance to use opinion surveys and the like. They are dismissed as unnecessary and a waste of money because 'we know what the people want'.

In a diverse and plural society, with all its complexities, the simple mechanism of the ballot box, important though that is, begins to look a bit inadequate. Local authorities have had to come to terms with protest and with pressure groups. The need now is to find better ways of bringing citizens and their views and knowledge more openly into the processes of policy formation, decision-making and, of course, performance review — without in any sense undermining the role of the councillor as elected representative. Not only would this strengthen representative democracy, but it should also make local government seem more open and rooted in its locality and serve to strengthen people's identity with its institutions.

There is then a further issue. The traditional emphasis has been on representative democracy but there is also potential for developing ways of allowing ordinary citizens to *participate* in decision-making. That means sharing power in defined spheres of activity. Decentralisation and the use of some kind of neighbourhood focus to which particular matters are delegated is one example; the statutorily required devolution from the LEA to school governing bodies is another; the use of co-option to bring representatives of community interests on to council committees is another. There are some statutory constraints but there is more potential than most people would admit. Such devices can enrich both decision-making and citizen involvement.

The sceptics will talk of apathy and disinterest. The emergence of successful school governing bodies and a new group of highly motivated and dedicated participants — witness the reaction of school governors to education spending cuts — gives lie to this. There may be scepticism and cynicism about involvement in consultative machinery when, it seems, the consultation counts for little. The picture looks quite different when there is a job to do, and where there is a genuine attempt to involve for real rather than symbolic reasons.

In short, **serious attention needs to be given to ways in which representative democracy can be strengthened by bringing a wider range of views, knowledge and judgement into the process and also to ways in which power can be shared not least at the immediate local level, with particular interests or in the management of services and institutions.** This issue is important not just for local government and its future. It also has implications for the wider issues of governance. The more that there is a sense of involvement in local government and the more people who are genuinely involved the stronger will be its role in — and the legitimacy it brings to — local governance.

HOW TO USE THIS CHAPTER

- Are there clear objectives and understandings about the roles elected members play? Are these roles supported by the council's various political processes? Are there gaps? What changes would make the political processes more effective?

- How does the party group machinery work? Is it open or does it cut across the formal structures and processes?

- How do the council and its decision-making processes relate to the wider world of local governance? How could the relationship be improved?

- Are there structures and processes which bring together the council and its political leadership with other leaderships in the locality? Which are these? What is the best way of doing this?

- Are there ways in which local democracy might be strengthened in your locality? Either by supporting and strengthening representative democracy or by finding ways of allowing other people to participate in decision-making? What are they and how could proposals be developed?

5

Purpose and direction

- Sense of purpose.

- Strategy and strategic management.

- Strategic approach to local governance.

- Planning, research and intelligence.

- Lateral approach to policy and action.

- Role of the centre.

The words 'strategy' and 'strategic' are probably the most over-used in the contemporary management lexicon. Everything is 'strategic' and everyone wants to be handling 'strategy'. In meetings the word will be heard many times — with many different meanings. The response of the sceptic will be that there can be no substance, words to hide behind, to cloak lack of grasp or ability, or a pretext for not doing the real job. Yet there is something very important here.

In a rapidly changing environment there is a need to make sense of what is happening and to ensure that the organisation stays on top of change — or, at least, does as much as it can to ensure that it has as much freedom to shape its destiny as possible. Equally, there is a need to prevent day-to-day pressures simply taking over. The operational demands on a local authority, particularly in terms of its day-to-day service provision, are enormous. For politicians and managers alike the temptation to be seduced by these and to lose sight of the wood for the trees is considerable. At the same time, in the complexity of the council's organisation and activities it is easy for staff to have little sight of what the council is trying to achieve and so of their place in it. What is true for insiders is likely also to be true on the outside; public understanding will be limited. How do we make sense of all of this?

For any organisation a sense of direction is important; for there will be some things which are more important to one organisation than others, but for all there will be major pay-off from the ability to focus. The scale and scope of change simply serves to emphasise the point; the more complex, and rapidly moving, the environment of an organisation the more crucial these things become. The local authority is no exception.

Behind the loose language and, indeed, the hype of the management textbooks there are some relatively simple messages. We will start with three of them. One is about setting purpose, the second is about developing strategic management and the third is about developing the organisation — and people — to sustain the approach. The three overlap.

❏ Sense of purpose

Organisational leaders have an important task in giving or, rather, defining and articulating a sense of purpose. Research shows that successful organisations are ones which know where they are going or what they are trying to be, and have a purpose with which staff can identify and which serves as a source of motivation or spur to action. Local authorities are no different. Like other organisations, they may well find it helpful to develop a set of words which captures this. This will probably combine some sort of statement of ambition with a set of values. Together the words should be able to capture the attention and interest of these working for or with the organisation. They need to be broad enough to allow space for the various parts of the organisation to set about the job of interpreting, translating, and refining the words to suit their own operational circumstances. In other words, such a statement needs to be owned by the whole organisation.

Put in these terms, it all sounds very easy. It is not — and local government introduces its own complications. To start with, a sense of purpose has to fit with the politics (usually party driven) as well as the organisational imperatives of the local authority. Its construction therefore has to involve both elected members and managers. Not that it will be highly political, but rather what the organisation is doing and where it is going is set within the council's political objectives. Secondly, a local authority is a complex organisation with a whole range of different functions and responsibilities. A multi-purpose organisation will have difficulty in defining purpose in a way which makes sense to all its different parts. Different services may often seem to be pulling in different directions. Something is needed which has integrity in itself and makes sense to all, but which can be amplified and filled out, department by department. The public nature of the local authority also means that it needs to communicate with and hold the attention of its outside world.

That tells us that sense of purpose will be more general than specific, simple than sophisticated, leaning towards the language of slogan rather than the committee report. People, inside and outside, will not easily identify with detailed policy statements or planning documents. The objective here is to produce something round which there can be a kind of instinctive coalescence: 'that's what we are about', 'these things drive our organisation', 'it has the hallmark of our council'. Identity with it should then help to drive the organisation — and make it understandable to the outside world.

But, of course, having such a statement is only a start. To leave it at that is pointless, and bad practice; it needs to be tested in action. Organisation and people need to be capable of delivering it and sustaining it. We shall return to this. Experience shows that for every good example of a statement of value and purpose driving a council in what it does, there are others where something has been produced but with no effect — save that it withers and is forgotten. **Organisational leaders (politicians and officers) need to define a sense of purpose in the organisation, identify key values for it and then follow it through in what they do.**

❏ Strategy and strategic management

A sense of purpose can give an outline shape or provide a foundation for what a council is about, but it can only go so far. It is then necessary to go on and develop a way of sorting out the key areas of change from the day-to-day routine, decide how to respond to them and then build the capacity to deliver. Two things about this. First, there is nothing new in it. There have been successive attempts over the years to find approaches which give greater order or rationality to the management of what otherwise seem extremely messy conflicting demands and pressures and usually piecemeal reactions. The attempts have tended to fail, either because they have been all-encompassing and over-ambitious and or because they have assumed a high degree of certainty about the present and future, when there is often precious little certainty, and so been blown off course.

Secondly, we need to accept that however rational and well-ordered we may want to be, there are major limitations. Everyday problems and crises will always be there to be dealt with — and properly so. Precisely because the local authority is there to make choices and to resolve the conflicting interests and demands of a plural society, it will be torn in different directions and will often be unable to act in what might seem a wholly consistent way. And then there is the obvious fact that many of the things which shape its action or demand a response are outside the local authority's control.

There is nothing peculiar in all of this. All sorts of different kinds of organisation would recognise much of it. Yet most would still want to ensure that they are in as much control as possible. There are no magic or simple solutions. The muddle of ordinary day-to-day life is not going to disappear because of a new management approach but it is that muddle which makes having a compass important. The challenge for any organisation is to find ways of creating space to set direction and concentrating attention on key themes or issues on the way.

These themes or issues are best thought of as the elements of change which cannot be coped with in the ordinary way, and which are going to require the organisation to change the way it operates, is structured or whatever. This is important. Much change can be handled incrementally and is simply absorbed into the organisation in the ordinary course of events. Some things are bigger. It is those which are the challenge and, of course, in many cases they will be the product of the changes we identified in Chapter 3. The precise approach or the processes which an authority adopts to give it some leverage over this 'strategic' change will vary according to local circumstances, style and so on. Suffice it to say that there will be some core elements — and roles for both elected members and officers. They include the following:

Review

However it is done there will be a need to review and map the environment, tracing out the various strands of change likely to hit the authority. There may be changes in the world at large (the 'external' changes of Chapter 3), changes affecting local government prompted by legislation, national government policy, changed public attitudes and the like. Alternatively they may be essentially internal things, led by local manifesto commitment or a determination to mount a major new initiative (e.g., the introduction of an equal opportunity policy or the development of an integrated policy for a particular client group).

Such a review process involves being as exhaustive and comprehensive as possible. The job is to build up as complete a picture as possible at this stage, rather than to home in on particular things. It can be undertaken in all sorts of different ways. At the end of it, the results have to be assembled in a digestible form for use at the next stage so that it is available to help people understand the complexity within which they are operating. The review of the environment then needs to be supplemented by a review of organisational strengths and weaknesses and its ability to respond. This stage of the process is more likely to be undertaken by officers, though member involvement may help when it comes to the next core element.

Judgement, selection and choice

The elected members play a key role in this, even though senior managers are likely to be involved in the deliberation which lead up to it. From the map of changes which has been constructed it will be necessary to select those things which members see as:

- most critical for the council;

- vital to get right and deliver on;

- dependent on significant change in the organisation and on which measures (time, management, money) will be focused.

These are the strategic issues. They are going to be limited in number (the capacity of an organisation to handle large scale change is limited). 'If everything is strategic nothing is strategic' is an epigram worth remembering.

Here again we need to remind ourselves about the real world. However well complexity is reduced to the simple, reality will have the habit of doing the unexpected. Thus review and selection cannot be seen as once and for all processes. To some extent they are repetitive or continuous. While their point is to bring some order and to allow concentrated effort, change itself is continuous, the 'map' will change and the strategic agenda may need adjustment. The objective of selection, remains the same: it is deliberately to reduce the uncertainty and create the conditions for concentrated and extended effort.

Setting the agenda

The issues will need to be explored. Whatever issues are selected, the next stage — involving both members and officers — is to put some shape on what has to be done and begin to be clear about how performance is to be assessed along the way. As with any such exercise, there is balance to be achieved between being hard-edged about timescales, objectives and targets and leaving space to explore and adapt. The nature of the issues will almost certainly dictate that new ground has to be trodden and new processes or structures or ways of working found. A key interim in setting the agenda will be to assess the capacity of the organisation and its resources, discover its strength and weaknesses in relation to the issues concerned. It is important to be clear both about how these can be built on or made good and what other relevant capacity or resources may lie in neighbouring organisations and the community at large.

Delivery

The heart of strategic management is to deliver successfully and secure the strategic change concerned. Again, this sounds obvious, but how many times have such attempts failed because inadequate attention has been given inside the organisation to delivering properly? This takes us back to our original definition. The real change problems come not from those issues which can be handled incrementally within the organisation, but from things which require a significantly different approach. Unless care is taken to create the capacity to be different, failure or — at best — only partial success will inevitably follow. Developing the organisation and its management (including, sometimes, its political management) is thus a key part of the whole. As this happens and as the new approach or way of working or whatever it is takes root, then the organisation will have shifted and what was strategic will become the new routine. While the weight of much of this work will lie with officers, members will maintain a key interest in its oversight and in ensuring that the agenda is delivered.

Monitoring and review

As delivery happens and as the strategic moves to the new routine, so it is important to monitor and review progress. The results of this need to be fed back so that there is learning and adjustment.

Talking in these abstract terms is not difficult. Putting them into practice certainly is. The logic for developing an approach which sorts out the more significant changes from the less significant and then concentrates on securing the change is powerful: it should give the organisation more leverage over how it responds, yet it is surprisingly difficult. The experience of numbers of local authorities who have tried suggests some important pre-requisites:

- Commitment from the political leadership and senior management and a determination to deliver.
- Champions who will keep up the pressure to make sure something happens.
- Determination to stick with it.
- Selectivity for the reasons which have been given.
- Protection of organisational time and space to make sure that the process is not crowded out by day-to-day demands and pressures.
- Some dedicated source for its purpose. While the chief executive and political leadership will make a critical contribution, they cannot do it

all. To keep things moving, assemble the required intelligence and information and monitor progress, there needs to be responsibility properly defined and allocated.

- Recognition that people and organisation matter and that the kind of changes involved will only be met successfully if there is effort to align skills, attitudes and behaviours and make sure processes and structure underpin and don't cut across what is desired.

Three other points are worth making. First, looked at in this way the distinction between what is strategic and what is not is demystified. There is nothing 'better' about one than the other. Routine or operational management is important in its own right and does not take second place. Secondly, while strategic management has been presented in terms of the whole organisation, the basic processes can be applied at any level or sub-set of the organisation. Thirdly, while the words will doubtless continue to be over-used and abused, we can begin to make better sense of them. The *strategic issues* are those which are selected; *strategy* becomes the framework which is developed to handle those issues; and *strategic management* is the whole process or approach including the implementation and delivery of change. All of it, to repeat the basic point, is concerned with those changes which demand a new response, and are incapable of being contained within the routine operations of the organisation.

Given the scale and significance of the changes affecting local government it is important **to develop processes of strategic management. That is, of reviewing the sources and pressures of change, identifying and selecting for special attention those which will cause the organisation to act differently, determining how to deal with them, and seeing the change through, especially in terms of organisation and management development.**

❏ A strategic approach to local governance?

We have talked of strategic management for the local authority itself. The local authority is then part of the wider pattern of governance in the locality — with others playing their individual part and sharing in responsibility. The possibility obviously arises of the same kind of approach being taken to the wider local agenda.

Local governance is self-evidently complex. It draws attention to the fact that many organisations are involved in shaping the local community, its public provision and its common good. All or most of these organisations will have clear and limited purposes and thus be able to get on with their own job. However, as we have seen, the nature of many issues makes collaboration necessary to make and shape provision (e.g. care of the elderly, provision for young children, support of the unemployed, etc.). Collaboration is also needed to tackle the 'wicked' issues which pay no respect to organisational boundaries but which are important in the life of the community.

There is thus no single focus — let alone institution — of local governance. In Chapter 4 we noted the need to underpin collaborative relationships with a degree of formality of structure or focus. When limited partnership or common action between a well defined set of partners is concerned this may not be difficult. Where issues are looser and possible collaborators less well defined there will be more of a challenge.

There are wider possibilities. The arguments about change in the local authority can also apply to a whole locality. That is to say, some changes will be more significant than others in terms of scale and impact; some will be capable of being handled without too much difficulty within the ordinary run of formal and informal arrangements; and some will not — or, at least will be better handled with new approaches, ways of working and so on. Just as a single organisation can be encouraged to create and protect space and time to review, choose and see key issues through to delivery key issues, so can a wider locality. At the same time, the capacity of the locality to work together can be built and can give form to an important part of the process of local governance.

Some of the attempts at partnership, particularly in the economic and social regeneration field, have discovered this. They have, perforce, had to identify key problems and issues to be tackled, develop a shared understanding about how they should be tackled and agree who does what. The development of urban policy inspired this kind of approach in City Challenge; it has been taken a stage further in the City Pride experiment. In the latter case three cities were asked — local authorities working with their communities — to identify a ten year vision and set about establishing how it might be implemented.

The experiment is still in its early days. Where it will lead to remains to be seen, and whether it was properly thought through in advance is an open question. Like some other less formal partnership ventures it offers some clues:

- a board had to be created bringing together the local government interest with other public agencies, the private sector, voluntary and community interests;

- a 'prospectus' had to be prepared articulating a shared vision for the city concerned;

- this had then to be worked through in terms of implementation and the part the various actors could play.

In at least one of the cases this process was extended to include:

- a process of detailed dialogue and consultation with the various sectors, using focus groups open meetings and the 'umbrella' organisations;

- public consultation through public meetings, consultation documents, the local media and general debate;

- an examination of trends and changes and selection of a core list of major concerns if the city was to respond properly to what was happening to it and manage change, using away days for detailed discussion, research and the results of consultation;

- concentration on those strategic issues identifying what needs to be done, by whom and with what enhancement of capacity, through detailed dialogue with the agencies and organisations (public, voluntary and private) involved.

While there is no one model or route to be followed slavishly, if sense is to be made out of the complex web of participants and relationships in local governance, establishing dialogue and regular exchange and developing a shared understanding and vision for the locality is a good starting point. The stages of the strategic management approach which we have described provide an appropriate framework for the task. Of course, there are lots of dilemmas and questions:

- The local authority has a key role but it is only one player among many.

- What legitimacy does the process have?

- How is representativeness to be ensured? Assuming only a limited number of people on 'the board', how are they to secure the support of their constituencies?

- Commitment is key; how is this secured from all involved, and maintained?

- There is little point in the exercise if it stops short of implementation. Different organisations operate with different time horizons and, indeed, different degrees of freedom. What are the chances of pulling it all together?

- There is a danger of the process becoming the preserve of a local elite or establishment. How is this best prevented?

- Inevitably, conflicting sets of values and interests will be exposed. How can these be reconciled or real choices made — and accepted without an all-encompassing democratic forum?

Probably, the only thing is to recognise and accept such dilemmas and questions at face value and seek to deal with them as progress is made. Assuming that the idea of local governance is not a miasma, then ways need to be found of giving it reality beyond the action of its component parts. Exploration and experiment are needed: identifying strategic issues and seeking to create a shared understanding, agenda and commitment to create the capacity to implement are a good starting point.

Two provisos are worth entering at this point. First, that any attempt to put form into the process will run the danger of creating yet another organisation and yet another set of constraints in an already complicated situation. Some kind of minimalist organisational arrangement may well be necessary to drive and support the exercise — but that is all. Secondly, while the shared agenda needs to be collectively 'owned' by all involved, implementation can be driven in a pluralist, differentiated way. That is to say, individual organisations or specific partnerships or coalitions can pick up the various parts. Sustainable capacity is what is needed, not administrative tidiness. The 'board' needs to do no more than exercise collective oversight and review. In Chapter 3 we spoke of 'thinking local governance', that perhaps needs to be extended to 'think plural organisational arrangements'! One particular danger needs to be watched for: it is easy for enthusiasts and not the whole organisation to own this kind of external strategic activity. It is vital to guard against this and make sure that the right internal connections are made.

In the search for the meaning and development of local governance, consideration therefore should be given to developing a strategic approach. That is to say, ways need to be found to shape a common agenda of change issues for the locality and to determine how these can be handled and change delivered calling on the community's collective resources.

❏ Planning, research and intelligence

The discussion of the strategic management approach may have seemed to give short shrift to attempts to introduce planning frameworks into the management of local government. Something more needs to be said about this. Any attempt to plan, let alone indulge in the review and analysis which underpins the strategic approach, either inside the local authority or within local governance, requires a capacity for research and intelligence. For many organisations this is a *sine qua non*. For local government it is too often neglected, particularly in the face of resource-constraining decisions and cutback in basic support services.

Strategic, corporate or policy planners (the labels vary but the tasks are fairly similar) have often gained a loud name over the years because either:

- they have assumed too great a degree of certainty; or

- they have been too comprehensive or all-encompassing; or

- they have ignored or trespassed too far into the preserve of the relevant professionals; or

- they have argued simplicity where there is complexity; or

- they have just been too threatening as 'outsiders'.

This in turn has given the idea of forward planning a bad name. This is unfortunate — though the bad name has then been bolstered by arguments about the (inevitably short) timescales of politicians, the advantages which came from ambiguity and the freedom to 'muddle along', and the impossibility of local government thinking ahead when it is so constrained by central government policy and the vagaries of the annual RSG settlement.

Two, rather different, points are worth making. The first is that there are two senses in which planning is important. The first is that it is a corollary of the strategic approach already outlined. Determining what has to be done and delivering implementation implies planning. The other sense is that, both in a situation of scarce resources and one where many of the issues facing a local authority are long term in nature or involve long lead times, planning becomes an essential management tool.

That is not to say that a single view has to be taken about what will happen, what resources will be available and what action is needed. A number of private and of public sector organisations have demonstrated how uncertainties can be built into a planning framework and a range of scenarios

71

developed. This is essentially about constructing a series of 'what if' pictures and thinking through, setting out alternative patterns of circumstances and events. This can be done as a paper exercise, but it is also possible to do it collectively using conference style techniques and even stimulation. However it is approached what is important is that both politicians and managers accept the need to think in the medium and longer terms as well as within the confines of the electoral cycle and the budget cycle. Neither can be discounted, of course, but trade-offs can be confronted and pursued. It requires will, determination and understanding — but it is important and worthwhile.

The second point is about the role of the 'planner'. Whatever the criticisms of the past, there is major organisational benefit to be gained by having a person/people who lie outside the conventional disciplines, whose remit is to think differently and who are not part of the organisational establishment: people who are, thus, mavericks inside the organisation and who can act as grit in the otherwise smooth-running machine. These are people who, among other things, can also support the strategic management process — providing, of course, that they can connect properly with the organisation and their colleagues.

There is a separate debate to be had about who these people are and where they come from (dedicated appointments or secondments?), how far their remit runs (the relationship between the corporate centre and individual services) and how they are structured and operate. These are second order questions. The important thing is that the resource exists — whatever the size of the organisation. It is as much an issue for the new post re-organisation councils as for the longer established ones.

This then begins to dovetail with the research and intelligence capacity. Whether or not the people are the same, the local authority needs the capacity to assemble information and intelligence about its environment and about its own activities and capacity. How the research and intelligence function is structured and where it is located are again second order questions. Once again there are a couple of important points to be made.

First, there is no reason for the local authority to be self-sufficient. While it may want to attend to some of the data gathering and analyses from within its own resource (for reasons of confidentiality or confidence) there will be a range of external organisations already in the research and intelligence business (for their own domestic purposes) or well-placed to collect and supply (e.g. educational or research institutions). Thought thus needs to be given to making sensible use of the total resources available.

This point is reinforced by the second. In so far as research and intelligence activities are needed to feed the processes of local governance there is strong reason to work collaboratively in this area, minimising duplication and building complementarity. Private, public and voluntary sector organisations will all have a stake here. An important step to creating a shared understanding and a shared agenda may be to create a common information base and so share these resources. The proviso of course is that the same organisation may compete or conflict as well as collaborating. Providing this is recognised, pooling and sharing of resources can still be taken a long way.

While there may be criticism of the way in which policy/strategic/corporate planning has performed in the past this does not deny the importance of its potential or **the need to think about policy development for the medium and longer term as well as the short term. Similarly, it is important to recognise the role of the policy planner as 'maverick' or lateral thinker and facilitator of strategic processes. Research and intelligence are also important as support to these same processes.** Both have a wider relevance as we consider another aspect of the way the bigger policy picture is put together.

❏ A lateral approach to policy

Having a sense of purpose and taking a strategic approach to issues of change are important for any organisation, not least for a local authority or in the wider local governance. There is another important consideration when it comes to developing policy, managing delivery and dealing with day to day problems; that is to ensure that problems and issues are dealt with, as far as possible, as a whole and not fragmented unnecessarily by organisational boundaries. We shall turn to fragmentation and differentiation in the next chapter but there is one particular aspect worth picking up here. It is important both to the local authority and the wider patchwork of local governance.

Local authorities, like most large organisations, are divided into (vertical) chunks usually matching particular areas of service or function and professional disciplines. Such a functional division makes good common sense and is convenient. Historically, such sub divisions have often grown used to working independently of one another — education dealing with the education services, social services with the personal social services, housing with housing and so on. This is despite the fact that the real problems individuals may have involve more than one service. The problem is further compounded by the two tier system and by the fact of many key areas of public service being outside local government. However obvious it may seem, making the lateral connections between departments and organisations with overlapping interests and responsibilities has never been simple or easy. Some of the success stories of community care, bringing together social services and housing interests in the local authority with the relevant parts of the NHS, show what can be done but are more the exception than the rule.

A new dimension has then been given to the problem by the growing number of 'wicked' issues, the policy issues which have no regard for organisational boundaries and which demand a co-operative response across boundaries. **There is thus a pressing need to develop an organisational capacity to make the lateral or horizontal connections (within and between organisations) and to treat policy issues and operational problems as 'wholes' and not as something divided up for the sake of organisational convenience.**

To do this successfully means resisting all the in-built temptations to think *within* organisational boundaries and to place a high value on sole ownership of policy thinking and action. Straightforward as it sounds it does not come naturally to most organisations. Yet the elderly or confused person needs help, not trouble with the boundary between health and social services. The displaced or broken family is unaware of the niceties of the social services, education and housing divide — let alone where the social security provisions of the benefits agency or the probation service or responsibilities for job placements and training come in. Equally, citizens interested in the quality of the environment, public safety or a stronger local economy are not impressed by the argument that action is difficult or impossible because responsibilities are split.

Habits of mind which instinctively think laterally and people who are used to working across organisational boundaries (internal and external) are needed. In some cases, structural solutions may look tempting (for instance, within the local authority, reorganising with a lateral focus on client groups rather than a vertical one on services). They are usually misleading, because they simply bring into play new sets of boundaries and new problems.

More important are processes which themselves encourage new ways of thinking and working. These may be formal, i.e. creating mechanisms which force issues on to a joint agenda or enable two separate organisations to work easily together (e.g. creating a forum to bring together interests in public safety or the environment). They may also be informal: creating opportunities for people to meet and mix across organisational boundaries so that working relationships, when they are required, follow almost naturally. What is important is to recognise that working and managing across boundaries — essential though it may be — is different to working inside organisations.

74

Skills and behaviours will be subtly different and there will be a need to understand other organisational cultures, conventions and perspectives. As we say later, this both places a new demand on training and development and provides an opportunity for training and development programmes to directly facilitate better working relationships.

The need to make lateral or horizontal connections is not peculiar to local government or to public management. It may be helpful to look further afield at how the problem is tackled. Once any organisation has put into place a functionally based structure it will face the difficulties of putting the pieces back together again as it tries to see a 'whole' problem or issue. This may be a useful topic to reflect on with managers of other organisations in the locality. The linking of research and development to production in manufacturing firms, public health and the specialist disciplines of medicine in the NHS, Railtrack and the operating companies on the railways — indeed anywhere we see the 'left-hand–right-hand' issue — are examples. The experience is the same; the need for processes and procedures, attitudes of mind and the importance of recognising people collaborate well.

❏ The role of the 'centre'

There will be more to say about the role of the 'centre' later. However, in this chapter we have already begun to spell out an agenda. Recent years have seen many councils begin to re-define their role and some radically to change their structure.

In the past the centre did three things. It provided support services corporately and to the services departments. Secondly, it used these support services (notably the finance function, the personnel or establishment function and the committee clerk's role) to control. Information flowing into the centre provided a powerful lever, as did the requirement to gain approval to this or that action. Thirdly, it was the centre that usually took or led corporate initiatives. Together these things provided much of the glue which held the local authority together.

The big change has been to see clearer distinctions begin to emerge between the strategic or corporate role and the provision of support services (and also to see the shift of emphasis away from control to a more facilitative support — albeit with continuous oversight for legality, integrity and financial probity). CCT and LMS in particular have served to change the relationship between service-providing departments and institutions and central support services. Concern for overheads and the growth of various forms of contractual relationship have forced the pace. The trend to devolve management responsibility has aided the change: finance and personnel officers have been outposted to departments. The prospect of white collar CCT has introduced further turbulence and caused, not least, some pulling back from devolved arrangements. That will not stop support service customers increasingly calling the tune and having support services tailored more and more to their requirements. This is a far cry from even ten years ago.

It is the strengthening of the strategic role of the centre which is more important to us here. We have spoken of the need to lead and support the definition of purpose and strategic management, the making of lateral connections in both policy and operations and, of course the involvement of the local authority in local governance. All of these things require a wide involvement — and ownership — across the authority; they also require a motor which drives them. Leading members play a key part in shaping them and other members will have an interest and involvement. Joint working is needed across the officer–member divide. The centre thus looks both ways — into the organisation and as a vital link into the member area. The Chief Executive should be the pivot. She or he is, above all, a strategic manager and should have:

- ability to hold and help shape a view of the whole;
- an understanding of the forces of change and the ways in which the authority has to change;
- a grip on key policy areas and an awareness of lateral or horizontal linkages;
- ability to read and understand the organisation;
- sensitivity to and appreciation of the political world and the priorities, needs and demands of the elected members;
- ways of effectively linking the politician and the organisation together;
- a good understanding of the wider world of local governance;
- ability to spot and respond to gaps and to opportunities for new initiatives;
- ways of underpinning the local authority's leadership role and generating trust and confidence in its contribution.

Two things about this. The first is that it requires good working relationships with the political leadership. It is no coincidence that anecdotal evidence points to the powerful influence of chief executives and leaders who can and are able to work closely together. Such relationships are not necessarily easy and democratic processes can easily intervene and upset them. The relationship has to be such that it can continue regardless of the personalities of those involved.

The second is that while the spotlight has been placed on the chief executive (and no question but that role is key) there is more to the strategic centre than one person. There are two requirements, both of which should be obvious. First, there needs to be support. The role of the policy or corporate planner and of research and intelligence staff has been emphasised, as has been the need to feed the strategic management process. There is no single model of how to do it (there can be more or fewer staff, with wider or narrower responsibilities, on full time permanent contracts or secondment and attachment, or a mixture) and no single set of labels to use. All that is important is that there is a dedicated resource to call upon and use and which will challenge established patterns, ask awkward questions and so on. Being iconoclastic is important — just as is the capacity to be accepted in order to influence, encourage, cajole and lead.

The second requirement is that the chief executive is not the only strategic manager. The centre has conventionally been thought of as the central departments, clearly distinguished from those managing and delivering services. This will no longer do. The chief executive needs to work with senior managers across the organisation, who also have a strategic role to play in the overall management of the organisation and who are able to link their service or function to the whole. This strategic responsibility needs to be more clearly recognised than it often is in chief officer appointments and accountability. Just as we are in the middle of the process of re-casting and re-defining the role of the centre, so we are also seeing new definitions of senior management posts and a stronger assertion of the strategic component. There are a number of examples of councils which have developed a 'strategic (officer) board' where its numbers share corporate and strategic responsibilities as well as having oversight of services. Sometimes this will match a similar political leadership group. There are examples, too, of the use of 'strategic' labels and symbols but where there is little or no substance. Form without substance is unhelpful.

Obviously there needs to be more than words; the strategic approach needs skills and perspectives which are different to those involved in managing a department. How the collaborative approach works and how people are actually grouped are subsidiary issues. Again, there is no one model. What is essential is that the strategic centre is more than just a front, that it has substance and that there are shared understandings about what it is for.

Beyond the strategic, the centre will obviously continue to have a responsibility to monitor and ensure regularity, legality and probity. However in its continued re-casting there will be **a need to ensure that it has the capacity to support and drive the organisation's corporate and strategic processes and that it is defined in such a way that it draws in key senior managers from across the organisation.**

HOW TO USE THIS CHAPTER:

- Has your council a clear sense of purpose or direction? Is it widely shared and understood? If not, what needs to happen?

- Are there processes which would be recognisable as strategic management? Do they make a difference? Where are the weaknesses? How might they be overcome?

- What are the possibilities for developing a wider strategic approach in the locality? Who would need to be involved? How might this happen? What would work best?

- Are there adequate research and intelligence resources to draw on — inside the council or in the locality? Are they properly used? Do they provide the kind of output which prompts forward thinking and planning?

- How good is your authority (or you) at making the horizontal connections inside and outside the organisation? What is needed to make this happen better?

- Is the 'centre' right? How might it be improved? What are the most important — and least important — things it does?

6

Organisational matters

Most local authorities regularly change their organisation charts and structures. Items appear regularly on committee agendas seeking approval for some sort of change or other. A conventional approach to dealing with new problems has been to tamper with the organisation. This may or may not be right for each case has to be judged on its own merits. However, anecdotal evidence suggests that very often the organisational change doesn't deal with the problem in hand. The change is approved and made; there are high hopes that things will be different; 12 or 18 months later there is a lot of head-scratching and a recognition that the problem is not solved.

A parallel characteristic has been the inclination to create new bits of organisation to deal with new issues as they have arisen without thinking through what the best form or approach might be. Or so it seems. New departmental units are tacked on to the organisation — the symbolism of a hierarchy of command and a separate label (preferably with a seat somewhere in a senior management group) is powerful and seductive.

Neither of these approaches shows much sophistication. Traditional structures and models of organisation have lived on, to the extent that early 20th century local government would recognise readily much of today's organisation. On the face of it there does not seem to have been much fundamental thinking about organisation. Yet, there have been some profound changes. Three will make the point.

The introduction of CCT has promoted a contract culture and fostered the purchaser/provider split — striking at the heart of the monolithic organisation, dramatically changing relationships between front-line services and their support, putting strong downward pressure on overheads, and encouraging an entrepreneurial and anti-bureaucratic approach. The requirement to devolve responsibility (and the fashion of doing so) is the second example. The education service, with the introduction of LMS is a striking example as are those councils which have gone seriously down the decentralisation route. The characteristics here have been the development of local organisational capacity, together with structures and processes to facilitate its operation, and a radically different 'centre'. The third example is in some sense the consequence of much of this (as well as a response to financial cuts) and is the attempt to simplify overall structures — often coupled with strengthening their 'strategic capacity'. This involves, variously, merging departments, going for flatter structures, moving away from traditional notions of hierarchy and command, creating top level management teams with chief officers freed up to take a more strategic role and so on.

These changes point to a high level of organisational turbulence in local government. Very often the changes are being tacked on to existing structures, which highlights the difficulty of taking a radical look at the basic assumptions and building blocks of the organisation — the degrees of self-sufficiency, the relevance of functional divisions and departments, the appropriateness of hierarchy, the right spans of control, the role of the centre and so on. The difficulty of taking a radical look is greatly exacerbated in the political environment of local government, where vested interests and, often, innate conservatism spill over into the political world. The search for new patterns and models is usually genuine but the absence of clearly established alternatives is equally marked. There are deep issues involved. This chapter will explore some of them.

❑ Organisation and purpose

We have come through a period when there has been a tendency to say that organisation does not matter too much. Any structure can be made to work. The important thing is to get the informalities (culture, relationships and so on) right and all else will follow. Without denying the importance of the softer side of organisational and managerial life, we are moving back to a recognition that organisation does matter. There are different forms and styles of organisation and each is more or less suitable in different circumstances and situations. There is a growing body of experience and a growing literature which assembles evidence to support this. The structure of an organisation and the way it works can easily shape the way problems and issues are perceived, the kind of solutions found to deal with them, and the way these are implemented.

This suggests the need to find the right balance in thinking about organisation. Although, as ever, the danger will be that the balance concentrates too heavily on the formalities of organisational life. **A way of getting the balance right is to try and make sure that organisation is always seen in terms of structures and processes and people** (with 'people' involving skills and capacity, relationships, culture and so on). The trick then, of course, is to try and work with a blank sheet of paper and to build up the kind of organisational arrangements which seem to best fit particular situations and sets of circumstances.

Of course the real world is not a blank sheet. For the most part, organisations already exist and provide the starting point, with all their constraints of people, assumptions and practices in place. Even where there are exceptional opportunities, like the creation of the new unitary authorities in Scotland, Wales and parts of England, it is not easy. People seem too ready to clone the old, to be trapped by old experience or simply to lack the will, ability or time to take a more fundamental look.

Members play a key role in putting their seal of approval — and thus influence — on the shape of the organisation. They, too, are trapped by experience and tradition, often lack the experience or knowledge to help them take a broader view and, as we have said, are often suspicious that change will, as they see it, marginalise their role still further. There are exceptions; examples of leading members who have driven fundamental review and change or who have provided the political will to support new approaches and ways of working. There is also the occasional blatant perversity such as the new council where the members' allowance system drove it to create as many committees as it could, each of which then had to have a department to match!

However difficult it is, it is important to try and take a fundamental look at the organisation and to question how it should be in order to be effective. This is made all the more crucial by the kind of changes which are taking place in local government. This was a central message of the 1992 Local Government Management Board report *Fitness for Purpose*. If the extent to which a document is purchased, copied and quoted is anything to go by then this was extremely well-received and highly influential. Like many simple messages,

- where market mechanisms are operating there must be provision for appropriate boards, or

- for delegation to local arrangements where there is decentralisation;

- local governance activities will require processes which will make lateral connections inside and outside the authority, both on the political and officer sides of the organisation;

- the balance between professional and generalist managers and culture will vary;

- conventional, hierarchical structures and bureaucratic procedures will remain important where there is strong emphasis on equity and fairness of treatment and in managing routine operations;

- such arrangements will not fit circumstances where there is strong emphasis on local discretion, development activities, partnership working, and so on where looser, less formal and more flexible structures and processes will be needed;

- skills will be different and need to be closely honed and related to different circumstances.

Complicated though the reality may be the essence is straightforward: **organisation (structures, process, systems and people) is important and needs to be designed and developed to fit its purpose(s).**

❏ Organisational fragmentation, differentiation and integration

Recognising that organisational arrangements are unlikely to be uniform, reminds us that in any local authority there will be internal differences and divisions. One of the consequences of much of the government's policy towards local government in recent years — and the legislation which has supported it has seen increased fragmentation. That is to say, a whole range of things have happened which have led to the break up of the organisation or, at least, introduced pressures in that direction. For example:

- CCT with its purchaser/provider split and DLOs and DSOs as contracting units;

- the wider contract culture with its business units;

- the requirement to devolve responsibility to school governors (LMS) and the trading relationships which result;

- the opting out provisions — schools, housing, etc.;

- partnership arrangements (city challenge, SRB initiatives and so on).

At the same time, of course, there have been fashions and ideas about good management which have pushed in the same direction, notably the pressures to:

- decentralise or devolve management responsibility within the organisation generally;

- emphasise clearly defined accountability and performance (for both individuals and groups);

- set up arms-length organisations — sometimes to underline discrete responsibility and sometimes as a way round legislative constraints.

The word 'fragmentation' is essentially negative and is often bound up with a political response to government action. This is an over-simplification and unhelpful. Undoubtedly some of the action the government has taken does have a down side and has had a negative impact on the organisation. However, the implication is that, before it happened, the local authority was an integral whole and behaved as such. That is, of course, nonsense. Any organisation of any scale or complexity builds into its structure some kind of *differentiation*: functional, geographical, disciplinary, etc. This is to make it easier to manage, to allow for specialisation or concentration of effort, to provide for greater identity between organisation and task and so on.

Traditionally, the strong differentiation in local government has been between services (with their supporting, professionally based, departmental structures and matching committees and powerful chairs) and between direct service delivery departments and central support departments (with their desire to control the organisation). Other forms of organisational differentiation, often within departments, but also on a geographical base, introduce further complication. Few authorities have found wholly effective ways of managing this differentiation and creating an integrated whole. Indeed, some chief executives will openly say that the new pressures — CCT, devolution, the contract culture and so on — have allowed them, for the first time, to get to grips with what they see as more insidious divisions.

All of this suggests a need to re-frame the language and approach. Recent changes have introduced new forms of differentiation into the organisation: of that there is no doubt. This means, in turn, finding new ways of managing differentiation even if the task is more complicated because the lines of differentiation are more complicated. Managing differentiation is about integrating where integration is necessary — for policy reasons, or to make operations and problem solving effective, or to maintain sufficient integrity in the whole organisation to allow for decisions to be made about priorities and for it to be able to act as a whole. Where integration is impossible, because differentiation is too deep, then there will be potentially negative and possibly serious dysfunctional consequences. *Fragmentation* is best left as a term to describe the negative situation of differentiation without the ability to integrate. The purchaser/provider split, locally managed schools, business units and so on do not necessarily mean fragmentation any more than the existence of housing, planning, education and social service departments do. They only mean fragmentation if integration is impossible.

To repeat, **the key to managing any organisation is to identify the ways in which it is differentiated, be clear where integration is needed (and why), and seek the means to provide for that integration. Only after that will it be clear if there is fragmentation; then the task is to see whether it is possible to make any kind of change which will overcome it.** Clearly what is true for the whole organisation will be true for any part of it which is itself differentiated.

Responsibility for this 'whole system' management lies with chief executives and senior managers (and the strategic or corporate centre of the organisation) on the one hand and leading politicians on the other. The latter have a dual interest: they have their own political structures and processes which are differentiated and need their own integrating mechanisms; they also have an interest in the strategic oversight of the whole organisation to ensure that it is performing and delivering their policies and priorities effectively. We have already argued the importance of political and organisational structures and processes which can take a strategic approach and make the necessary horizontal connections in policy and operational terms. The argument goes a stage further here by identifying the fact of many divisions and so, potentially, a wide variety of threads to be joined together. The ability to see the whole is very important.

Once again, to write in these terms makes the problem, and the possibilities, seem simple and straightforward. Yet they obviously are not — witness the fact that most local authorities are struggling and too many seem to give up and simply complain about the difficulties fragmentation presents for them. For some there may be political reasons for this but for others it is more a case of not persisting. Without in any sense justifying all that has happened or all the steps the government has taken, the reality is clear and there are new circumstances which have to be managed. Many of the new lines of differentiation are not suddenly going to go away — some may change and other ones will appear — and, anyway, most have benefits as well as disadvantages. And, of course, it is not all the consequences of external action. Quite a lot of differentiation results from voluntary initiative (e.g. devolved management, and decentralisation, much of the contract culture, new organisational forms such as business units, etc.). The question facing all authorities, regardless of the source of their differentiation, is how is the situation best managed? What are the means of integration?

The simple answer is that there is probably little or nothing which is not already in place somewhere or being experimented with. Having re-framed the debate to one of differentiation and integration, it is then a case of examining all the possibilities and seeing what best applies in any given case. Again it can be argued that the *means* of integration must fit the *purpose* for which they are intended. In doing this it will become clear that some ways of integrating will themselves introduce new lines of differentiation. For example, some councils have chosen to decentralise (differentiation) in order to integrate at the sharp end of service delivery; others have introduced new processes to deal with a particular issues or client groups (differentiation) in order to integrate their capacity to solve problems or meet particular needs.

Assuming that the search for integration is selective (i.e. for much of the time differentiated parts of the organisation can simply get on with their own work) the following are examples of approaches which can be used. They are drawn from the experience of three councils (a London Borough, a northern metropolitan council and a county council) all of whom have sought to be explicit about differentiation and integration:

- clear definition of strategic purpose/direction and of core values to give an overall framework for everyone;

- changing structure — but there are different ways (e.g. one brought adjacent services together into multi-purpose directorates and then differentiated responsibilities and tasks internally; another went for a highly differentiated structure, without over-arching directorates, to (a) concentrate attention and effort on well defined tasks and (b) make it clear when action — joint policy development, collaborative working, joint staffing arrangements or whatever — was needed to integrate);

- decentralisation to integrate at the neighbourhood level;

- adaptation of committee and political processes to create groups or panels able to work across boundaries and to strengthen (in two cases) the policy committee;

- joint arrangements to bring together the political and senior officer leadership to provide overview, encouragement and review;

- re-definition of the centre's role to provide stronger strategic capacity to identify/stimulate/monitor integration across the organisation and to determine what could be 'loose' and what must be 'tight';

- definition of common standards (financial, procedural, customer-focused etc.) which must be adhered to across the organisation and in relation to contractors and partners;

- monitoring and review of such standards and of integration generally in relation to performance;

- development of officer processes working parties, lead departments or officers, etc. to develop and manage integration of policy development or operations;

- leadership to shape a culture which puts high value on lateral thinking and integrative action;

- newsletters, briefings and use of other communications media to promote the whole organisation and publicise good integrating practice;

- training and development activities (especially management development) to build contacts, networks and linkages across the organisation;

- encouragement of social and other informal activity for the same reasons;

- use of secondments and attachments to strengthen links across boundaries and to bring new/lateral/integrating thinking and perspectives;

- development of career patterns which cross the organisation, again to strengthen integrating capacity.

The list can be added to. Clearly some of the above are short term tactics, others can only bear fruit in the longer term. They will serve different purposes and thus need selective and differential use. The skill is in deploying the right ones at the right time and in the right combinations. Managing differentiation and integration — and avoiding fragmentation as far as possible — is an important part of the management task. At the end of it all there will be some fragmentation — making some tasks very difficult.

❏ Local governance: differentiation, integration and organisation

We have made the point, in earlier chapters, that one of the reasons local governance has assumed great importance is because of greater external differentiation (and, potentially, fragmentation). Suffice it to say that similar issues of integration present themselves — and similar kinds of tactics (or variations on them) are available to deal with the situation. The situation is made that much more complicated by the fact that here we are obviously talking of separate organisations rather than parts of the same organisation.

In Chapter 4 we argued for the development of local strategy or vision as a basis for integrating activity in local governance and that formal structures and processes were needed to underpin joint organisational action. The above discussion points to the potential for using other approaches — formal and informal — in developing personal contacts and networks which will both encourage and facilitate integration. Joint training activity, management events, social interaction and the conscious attempt to open up at least temporary career moves via secondment and attachment will all help. The importance of re-defining local public management also underlines the importance of developing contact, identity and exchange.

With an eye to the organisational underpinning of local governance, it is worth making the obvious point that, again, organisational form and style will have an impact. Form must again serve purpose. A formal and bureaucratic organisation, with extended hierarchies and centralised decision-making will find it much more difficult to act than more open and flexible forms of organisation with the ability to devolve responsibilities and take risk. Similarly, the 'typical' bureaucrat will not be a good networker and is likely to feel distinctly ill at ease in this more fluid world, where skills of influence, negotiation and advocacy are at a premium, rather than ones suited to a framework of precedents, rules and control. In fact there is a real dilemma for many organisations. The person best suited to the arena of partnerships, networks and coalition building may be precisely the sort of person who is not a conventional organisation person and who thus sits uncomfortably within or representing a large organisation.

So far as local governance is concerned, then, the management agenda also needs to include getting the organisation (structures, processes and people) right to provide for integration in what is a highly differentiated world.

There are three other organisational matters which are important to touch on.

89

In some senses they are the consequences of what has been said so far. In others they are distinct.

❏ Managing organisational change

A common thread of the agenda is that there needs to be change in the way that local government is managed and organised. Some of that change will be small-scale, incremental, and reasonably easy to see through. Some will not. The impact both of the large scale changes described in Chapter 3 and, of pursuing some of the themes on this agenda will entail large scale change inside the organisation. Managing that change is a major exercise in itself. There are three particular aspects worth noting.

First, the nature of change itself. Listening to managers (and politicians) talking about change often leaves the impression that it is something limited and distinct, a one-off experience, or a necessary prelude to a new stability. Timescales are set and there is a language of 'destination' and 'completion'. Understandable though this is (it helps to put some certainty round uncertainty and define some temporal boundaries) it is highly misleading. The reality of the contemporary world — not least in local government — is that change is a continuing fact of life, as is uncertainty. While a particular change programme may be set out for a period of months or years, the certainty is that when it is complete — or more likely before — circumstances will have changed, new challenges thrown up and another round of change required. Difficult though it may be, **it is necessary to help organisations and people understand that continuous change, rather than 'one-off' change leading to a new stability will be the order of the day.**

It is difficult for two reasons in particular. First, because most of us prefer stability to upheaval; and second, because the very concept of change induces anxiety, insecurity and even fear. Such emotions lead people individually and collectively towards defensiveness rather than to a sense of excitement about new opportunities. Management has a responsibility not just to create an understanding about the continuing nature of change but also to try and create an environment which sees opportunity and excitement, not problems and a need to defend the status quo. Among other things, this means being alive to anxiety and insecurity and doing as much as possible to alleviate them.

The second issue is about time. An examination of the way many major change programmes have been planned and implemented (or inadequately planned but implemented) in local government shows that time is usually understated. This is, yet another very simple but important point. Generating major change takes time. It is not, as we have said, just about changing structure diagrams. That may be involved, but it is also about getting processes and systems right and, above all, about people. New skills may be needed; new understandings, attitudes and behaviour almost certainly will be; a matching culture is also likely to be needed.

None of these things happens overnight. They require careful preparation and the investment of a lot of time and effort. Unfortunately this has often been and *is* often, not recognised. Sometimes the pace is forced from the outside but often it is not. **Whatever the circumstances and from wherever the drive, it is essential to prepare properly and to provide sufficient time**. To get that wrong at best leads to frustration and cynicism about management capacity. At worse it will lead to major failure.

The third point is about the role of managers in leading and shaping change. A piece of research by MORI for the Local Government Management Board in 1991 on the management of change told a depressing story and confirmed much anecdotal evidence. To put it simply, managers managing change were not rated well. The criticisms were the obvious ones:

- lack of communication and information;
- lack of preparation;
- little attempt to gain an understanding of what change was about or where it was leading;
- lack of consultation;
- lack of listening to what the organisation was saying;
- inadequate care and attention for staff caught up in the change process.

While some of that may be an inevitable consequence of the change process and some of it without a great deal of foundation, at its heart is an obvious message: **a key part of managing and leading change is the exercise of good management and leadership skills** so that people are motivated, informed, understood and, as far as possible, committed to change, helping shape rather than obstructing it.

❑ Delayering organisations and defining management

One of the main strands of organisational change in local government involves 'delayering', 'down-sizing' and shortening or flattening hierarchies.

There are two prime motivations for this. One is to make organisations more flexible. The other is to cut out unnecessary bits and release scarce resources. The second is an important point which we shall return to in Chapter 8. Because of the significance of the trend and the pressure to be seen to be following it, it is worth touching on a few key issues which have wide organisational significance.

The first is about cutting out jobs. This may be important. The Audit Commission and others have drawn attention to the scope for it. Public organisations, like others, have had a habit of growing in an incremental and often unplanned way as new tasks have emerged. It is altogether unsurprising that organisations have 'fat' and, probably, unnecessary tiers. (The American concept of the 'thickening organisation' — which suggests that political, cultural and other intra-organisational pressures make it all too easy for hierarchies to extend and organisations to grow (without challenge) is a useful one as an antidote to simplistic ideas about lean organisations, not that either is right or wrong *per se.*)

Thinning them down and seeking to cut out 'fat' is reasonable — but with two big provisos. It is no good doing this without looking seriously at the work to be done and the processes used in order to re-design the jobs which are left. (Re-engineering, another fashion, takes us in that direction.) Too often, 'down-sizing' results in, yes, fewer people and tiers; but the people who are left are trying to cover the same ground and do all or most of what was done before. Equally, cutting out jobs and ignoring the need to have a capacity to innovate, develop new ideas or approaches, staff working parties and task forces and respond to new circumstances, is pointless. What might be described as institutional anorexia sets in, undermining the need to spot and do things differently. **Job — and process — design or re-design, should be an integral part of organisation re-thinking as should be balancing the capacity and purpose of the organisation in the process**. Arbitrary targets for cash or staff reductions, while they may concentrate the mind, may create a blinkered approach.

They may also give rise to another issue and one related to something we have already discussed. The temptation may be to take delayering, down-sizing or whatever it may be called, and apply it uniformly. Organisation needs to fit purpose and its shape will vary according to purpose. Some purposes and tasks may be more labour intensive than others and require the maintenance of a more traditional looking bureaucracy. Regulation and control functions and situations where fairness, equity, rules and precedents are important may demand larger numbers of staff and even additional tiers of supervision, because of the need to check, keep meticulous records and the like. The point must not be overplayed — it could easily become the defence for the indefensible — but it points to an important note of caution: **different parts of the organisation may require different intensities of staff support and require different supervisory structures because of the purposes they are serving.**

The third issue is about defining management and supervision itself. The last 20 years have seen enormous emphasis placed on management in local government in a situation where before the concept was almost totally absent. The language was of administration and entirely different. To be defined as a 'manager' has become important and a high value has been placed on 'managing' in the organisation. One consequence of this is that, during this time, the number of management jobs has grown considerably. It may just be that this has been without very careful thought or planning and that there are now too many of them. It is commonplace to hear senior managers or politicians complaining that the real resistance to change is among middle managers. Could it be because middle managers really do have something to fear from change?

There has been interesting comparative work on middle management in UK and German enterprises which reveals a point worth contemplating further. In Germany, few middle-managers see themselves primarily as managers. They see themselves as being involved in operational jobs first and foremost with a supervisory or managerial role added on. In the UK middle managers tend to see themselves primarily as managers. Admittedly the study was of private sector organisations but the results are thought-provoking. Have we got the balance wrong? Are there too many people dedicated to managing? and, if so, managing what? Should there be more emphasis on operational tasks with a lesser managerial or supervisory component?

This brings us back to another aspect of job design. In examining organisation structures and the roles within them **there is a need to pay special attention to defining managerial jobs, what management is required to do and how it is done.** The evidence suggests that in most organisations there may be difficult and very uncomfortable questions to be asked and answered. They will involve issues of relative status as well as job content.

❑ The learning organisation

The final point in this chapter takes us back to where we started. Whatever the purpose the organisation is serving — and thus whatever the pattern of structure, processes and people, whatever the pattern of differentiation and integration, and however it tackles the management of change, there is one imperative which remains constant. Government — and thus public management — is about learning, particularly about the environment which it shapes and to which it has to respond and about itself. Organisations must, therefore, have a learning capacity. Understanding what is going on in the external world, responding to day-to-day performance with its successes and failures, and watching the performance of other organisations are all part of the learning process. We shall return to this again in Chapter 8, but in the meantime there are some organisational points to be made.

There are two kinds of organisational learning. One accepts existing policies and plans and is simply a response to daily operation in terms of doing more or less (library opening times, numbers of school meals, staff to handle planning applications and so on). This is usually called 'single loop' or 'bounded' learning. More important is 'unbounded' or 'double loop' learning. The 'second loop' (unbounded by the constraints of the way things are done now) is about re-framing the situation. In the light of experience, are different policies, plans or activities necessary? This capacity to develop a new perspective and to re-frame issues, is obviously important in developing strategic processes, making lateral connections, and so on.

This kind of learning requires particular kinds of skills, and people can be encouraged and nurtured in a variety of ways. It also requires:

- an organisation which does not become enclosed in its own tasks, insulated from what is going on around it;

- processes which encourage review, and question (any organisation rests on sets of assumptions which can easily take over and prevent real exploration);

- sufficient flexibility to encourage and take seriously ideas which came from any level in the organisation;

- processes which allow those who work at the front-line to feed their experience to the top of the organisation and the top to listen to the front-line;

- a determination to devolve responsibility and discretion to allow managers and staff to respond to new circumstances and problems and to adapt to and work with adjacent organisations;

- a willingness to experiment (and to admit failure) and thus to encourage diversity;

- encouragement of networks across the organisation (and beyond) to by-pass or overcome organisational boundaries and barriers and to fashion different perspectives and approaches.

Quite a bit of this is about organisational and management development — and fits with the development of strategic and lateral approaches. What is important is the recognition that developing a learning capacity — or not — is a consequence of a series of organisational considerations. To put it another way, some patterns of organisational life (structures, processes and people) are more likely to facilitate learning than others. **Part of thinking through purpose, as the first stage of getting the organisation right, must be to determine the values to be placed on learning and the kind of learning which is important to the organisation.**

Essential though it is to think of this across and through the whole organisation (viz the importance of front-line staff), the commitment and example of senior management — and, indeed, political leaders — will be crucial. Senior members of an organisation often under-estimate their capacity for influence. There is now a great deal of evidence from all kinds of organisations to suggest that the way such people go about their work, their willingness to question, challenge and re-frame and the way in which management teams and the like operate will have a profound effect. Encouragement and example have a habit of breeding more of the same. A closed and routinised leadership, averse to risks and falling back on convention will tend to perpetuate itself. Why should the rest of the organisation be any different if staff feel they can have no effect?

HOW TO USE THIS CHAPTER

- How far do the various parts of your organisation really fit the organisation's purpose? Are structures, processes and people seen as part of the whole?

- What are the key dimensions of differentiation in your authority? Which are the most important? Are there adequate means for integration? Where is there fragmentation? What can be done about it?

- How good are you and your colleagues at managing organisational change? Is adequate thought given to planning, preparation and explanation? Is time under-estimated? Do you know what staff think and how they might improve the situation?

- How much attention is given to job design and re-design? Is enough notice taken of the different needs and circumstances of different parts of the organisation? Are management and management tasks properly thought-through and defined? Are there too many managers?

- Can your organisation be defined as a 'learning organisation'? What needs to happen to make it one (or a better one)? What can you do to help this?

7

Closer to the people

- Top-down versus bottom-up.

- Decentralisation.

- Local local governance.

- Different kinds of community and (local) civil society.

- Closer to service users.

It is easy to become over-concerned about the things that matter to the 'top' and the 'centre' of an organisation. Important as these may be, they are only one perspective and only one part of the agenda. The local authority, like any other organisation, exists to serve its public. This implies accessibility, responsiveness, sensitivity and such like. The way it interacts with its public — the people who use its services and to whom it is accountable — and how it seems from their perspective are important.

❏ Top-down versus bottom-up

There is a real paradox in the management of local government. The 'top-down' view is one which, comes naturally to many politicians in their direction of the authority, and to managers, who have grown up on the inside of the organisation and become at least partly insulated from the world outside. The 'bottom-up' view, however, is crucial if the shape of services and the way the organisations actually works are to be got right. Because this view is unlikely to come naturally, because it is likely to be filtered out in the internal administrative processes of the organisation, the paradox can only be resolved by making a conscious effort to be different. Many would criticise local government for having done too little of this.

It becomes increasingly important for three quite different reasons — all of which were touched on in Chapter 3.

- Most fundamentally, issues of social exclusion, of stress and strain in the fabric of local society and of weakening social cohesion are increasingly important. Political views will vary about the nature of these and of the best ways of dealing with them. A common thread is the need to address them by making sure that local government, and governance, in all that they do are both meeting real needs and working responsively and effectively. This means understanding local society and seeing the organisation from the outside in.

- For many there is concern, too, at the increasing evidence of cynicism and alienation from public institutions, not least local government and local democracy. The need to find ways of being closer to the people and of re-connecting citizens to the democratic process and to *their* local government and governance is also becoming increasingly important.

- Additionally, one of the characteristics of our contemporary society is the desire for goods and services which are tailored to individual requirements. We are no longer prepared to put up with the mass produced and the impersonal. We have got used to purchasing things which suit our individual needs and preferences from the private sector and want the same from the public sector. What the public wants and not what the organisation thinks it should have becomes more important.

The 'how' of this opens up a broad range of possibilities and we shall touch on a series of them here. As with the rest of our agenda there are no simple solutions or recipe book panaceas.

The boundary between the political and the managerial is a fine one. There are essentially managerial issues to do with the way the organisation operates at the sharp end but these stand side by side with issues about decentralising political power and sharing it with the local community. In between are a whole host of concerns about how the local authority finds out what people want, how it relates to voluntary and community groups and so on. Together, they point to the **importance of a shared understanding across the officer–member divide about where the council stands and what it is trying to do in shaping its relationships with its public and community.**

❏ Decentralisation

Nowhere is this need for shared understanding and for clarity of objectives more important than where decentralisation is concerned. Many councils have pursued decentralisation in one way or another — and the story is peppered with frustration, misunderstanding and, often, failure. The motive is usually to do with building a better, more responsive relationship with the public and integrating services at the point of delivery but, of course, the possibilities are endless and the potential implications enormous. Where there have been problems it is usually because there has been inadequate thought and preparation.

The issue has been given a new significance in the local government re-organisation in Scotland and Wales. In the former, each council is expected to present a scheme for decentralisation to the Secretary of State by spring 1997; in the latter a new council must produce a scheme if requested to do so. In England the issues will undoubtedly be on the agenda of the new unitary councils. It is also on that of many others as a result of the Local Government Review process, when bold promises were made about the way in which existing authorities could be made to work better. Many of the metropolitan councils and London Boroughs continue to wrestle with the issues.

It is helpful to distinguish between three sorts of decentralisation as the first stage in being clear about definition and objectives:

- decentralisation of management responsibility within the organisation;

- decentralisation of management responsibility to neighbourhoods or localities;

- democratic decentralisation to the neighbourhood or immediate local level.

The first two of these are more to do with increasing responsiveness and effectiveness and a managerial agenda (even if politically driven). The third is more to do with re-vitalising democracy and sharing power with individuals and communities. The second implies the first but both of these need to be seen as quite distinct from the third.

Experience tells us that whatever route to decentralisation is taken there are four key factors which need to be carefully thought through:

- The tension between the desire for uniformity and the need to accept the diversity which is part of the rationale for decentralisation, including political difference and diversity where democratic decentralisation takes place.

- The tight/loose dilemma — what must be held 'tight' at the centre (and why) and what can be let go, for the periphery to manage in its own way. The balance will vary from organisation to organisation (and is another variation on the differentiation/integration issue discussed in Chapter 6).

- The people consequences. New responsibilities will bring demand for new skills, attitudes and behaviour — each of which needs to be actively prepared for — and there will need to be shared understandings about what is trying to be achieved

- The costs. These will obviously vary, not least according to what is being done and how extensive the decentralisation being undertaken is. They will have to do with numbers of staff and the time and effort involved. They need to be explicitly taken into account and weighed against the benefits, which also need careful identification.

We look at the three kinds of decentralisation in turn.

Decentralisation within the organisation

We have already pointed to this as one of the trends of good management practice. Little needs to be said about it, save to make clear that it *is* a kind of decentralisation. While at one level it is straightforward, at another it represents a marked shift from the traditional, centralised hierarchies of local government. The objective is to push responsibility and discretion as far down the organisation as possible. It is a kind of domestic version of the subsidiarity principle (that decisions should be made at the lowest level possible and that superior levels should not take responsibilities to themselves without agreed good reason). That principle, incidentally, provides a good rule of thumb when thinking about organisation design.

The assumption is that such devolved responsibility will produce more responsiveness, that accountability will be strengthened and that resources will be more effectively managed and thus overall costs more easily controlled. To deliver, however, obviously requires the framework to be defined so that the ground rules (financial, procedural, extent of discretion, etc.) are clear and people know where they are. New responsibility and discretion will flow from this — the staff involved need training, and appropriate support. The diverse ways in which LMS was implemented is striking testimony to the importance of the latter. Some education departments were meticulous in their preparation and support; others were more cavalier and seemed to assume 'osmosis' was adequate preparation.

(Area) decentralised management

Here we are talking about decentralisation of service management to a defined local area. Again the motivation is usually to do with responsiveness and accessibility and, sometimes, service departments, but here there is a conscious attempt to co-ordinate and integrate provision at the most local level by bringing together the relevant personnel. Thus a local office covering a number of services and providing a single reference point for the locality will often feature. Sometimes, in shire county areas, this will bring together access to both county and district services. This sounds straightforward enough but many authorities have discovered the benefits are more elusive than they expect — not least because of the way in which ingrained ways of working are challenged. Experience suggests a number of conditions for success:

- The local physical (office) presence may be easy to establish; more difficult will be the range and content of its responsibilities. There is a difference for example, between such offices as access points and as the focus for decentralised management. The greater the range of services and the wider its remit the more satisfactory it will be to its users. The more comprehensive it is, the more difficult it will be to organise and the more trade-offs there will need to be between different departments and services.

- Its mode of operation requires a delicate balance to be struck. The organisation as a whole will find uniformity easier, which the rationale for decentralising is diversity. Too little discretion undermines the point of decentralising; too much undermines the purpose of the local authority. Although the approach of different services may vary, the balance from service to service needs to be similar.

- Decentralised operations need central support (and overview). However, this means facilitation and a willingness to let go, not control. Support services need to be enabling not constraining and, again, there needs to be clear definition of the boundary between the centre and the rest. White collar CCT and the perceived requirement to re-centralise in order to make contracts easier to construct and manage also needs to be thought through.

- The accent on co-ordination and integration puts a premium on services getting their local act together. This is likely to lead to staff working, or wanting to work, across normal service or professional boundaries and even to re-define problems presented to them for solution. Professional pride and conventional practice will be challenged and tensions will be likely to arise with 'conventional' professional interests defending their corner. Again the issue is about striking a new balance as the possibilities for generic working are opened up.

- Generic working and generally dealing with a multiplicity of services and problems in one office will increase the pressure on staff. Greater job satisfaction and commitment may result but the burdens and the need for appropriate skills training needs to be recognised.

- Demands for more staff at local level will almost certainly occur. These may be justified but experience suggests that they must be looked at alongside the structure and design of the central organisation, which should be capable of reduction if the design for decentralisation has been got right.

- A serious attempt to decentralise to local areas will demand a new culture and ethos of working which will be significantly different to the old. It will be complicated further in those (probably many) councils where there is selective use of decentralisation, with only some localities being singled out and thus effectively two organisations, having to operate side by side.

- The importance of being clear what the corporate policy framework is within which decentralisation takes place — what is 'tight' (e.g. financial procedures, equal opportunities or environmental policies, particular client group priorities, etc.) and what can be 'loose'.

Decentralised political management

Decentralisation can take place to a local or neighbourhood level without disturbing the basis of political power or touching political decision-making processes. Politicians must set the direction for the decentralisation process but they can then leave it to the managers to get on with it. At least, they can in theory. Very often though, the possibility of something more emerges. There is growing interest in political decentralisation — often as a result of apparent success at the managerial level but also because elected members can see that it is at the level of the wards and neighbourhood that they can have more impact on the delivery of service to 'their people' and so be involved in management.

Needless to say the problems are significant, even if the opportunity to give local political expression is attractive. To start with it is necessary to recognise that there are a number of different approaches to political or democratic decentralisation:

- Political decentralisation processes can be built into existing processes. For instance, a service committee can organise sub-committees or panels based on geographical areas, either alone or in tandem with other committees.

- The political processes of a council can be extended by creating new area committees either with membership drawn only from the council or by including other representatives from the locality (determined by election, co-option or appointment). Although, in this case, there will be a need to be clear about who can vote on what and when.

- Using either approach, the thrust can be about using such bodies as neighbourhood forums for consultation only, retaining full executive authority within the council's existing structures.

- Alternatively, the new processes can be executive, exercising authority within defined limits.

There is thus a continuum of possibilities ranging from a relatively modest set of arrangements within the existing structure with only consultative responsibilities, to a new structure with executive authority and external representation. The further a scheme is along this continuum the more obvious will be the central issue in political decentralisation: the sharing of power. Many elected members feel uncomfortable with this, while others see community empowerment as a key way to re-build a strong local government. Political values and preferences thus come into play. It is important that they are recognised and an explicit stance taken. To avoid confronting the issues but to move down a decentralising route is only to store up trouble for the future.

Being clear about the nature of political decentralisation is crucial. There are some other lessons which are well learned from those who have tried:

- It obviously does not make much sense to move towards political decentralisation without tackling management decentralisation first.

- Any steps taken will be high profile and very public. It may be difficult to turn back as expectations will have been raised.

- There may be party political issues to contend with. For example, local committees, drawn from local members, may have a different political balance from the council as a whole. This is not necessarily an insuperable problem — but it needs to be recognised!

Overall, decentralised arrangements, political and managerial, may well offer potential benefit in terms of responsiveness, access, co-ordination, a stronger local democracy, wider 'ownership' of the council's activities and so on. However it is easy for proponents to be starry eyed and not to recognise the pitfalls and problems as well as the benefits and opportunities. Many of the pitfalls are likely to be the result of muddled thinking and the lack of clarity. **Any move towards decentralisation, managerial and/or political, needs to be accompanied by clear thinking about objectives and about what needs to be done to make it work.** There are now enough examples of practice, to make it easy to tap experience to help this process.

❏ Local local governance

Getting closer to the people obviously embraces the possibilities for decentralisation within the local authority. There are wider issues when we talk of local governance. What is true for the whole local area is also obviously true for the localities or communities within it. Indeed, for some people the terms local or community governance have more to do with the very local area than the wider locality.

It is important to note that much that has been said can be applied to the more immediate or local level. A number of councils, either as part of their moves to decentralise or quite separately, have been experimenting with ways of bringing together the various key players at a level below the local authority as a whole — a neighbourhood or locality in a large urban authority; a small town or a village in shire areas. Concerns with governance at this level are more likely to have to do with operational issues in the delivery of service, local developments or local priorities than with the larger scale strategic agenda. That is not to belittle them; not least because it can be a way of giving local substance and reality to the broader agenda at local authority level.

Many of the most existing developments have been around initiatives to do with social and economic regeneration and community development. Particularly striking are those in which real voice and authority is given to local people — and where local authorities and other agencies have been prepared to 'let go' and adapt their own policies and practices to accommodate local initiative.

In many parts of the country, of course, this kind of local governance brings into play the relationships between the different tiers of local government (most obviously, county, district and parish) and the way they manage their relationships and affairs at the sharp end of operations. Protestations of good or improving relationships do not count for much if things do not work on the ground! Attempts to grapple with this dimension of local governance have also been given special impetus by the *Local Government Review* — promises having been made about improving the status quo which now need to be delivered.

Bringing together organisations and agencies at the most local level and working with them to the benefit of local people will not get far if local government cannot get its act together. Where relationships have been bad — or, simply, where there has been no reason to bother about them — action is needed. This may not be easy. **At the most local level, as with any kind of inter-organisational working, there needs to be clear understanding about working relationships, recognition of strengths and weaknesses and exploration and identification of areas for joint action**. This will involve explicit discussion of what is involved, confronting the difficulties and problems which arise. To hide from these may seem convenient in the short term; it will be damaging in the longer term. Clear understanding provides a foundation which can be built upon. The relationship *should* be driven by the realisation that the public are more bothered about the need for 'seamless' services than the niceties of organisational boundaries.

There are all sorts of devices which can be used to cement joint co-operation, especially between levels of local government:

- a jointly agreed protocol to define the nature of continuing relationships;

- a local charter defining what the public can expect of such relationships;

- joint member committees to plan or oversee areas of mutual interest and co-operation;

- joint arrangements for the management of contiguous service provision and responsibility (e.g. housing and social services, planning, environmental issues, etc.);

- delegation of responsibility from counties to districts (or either to parishes) for particular duties and functions or 'purchasing' arrangements which produce the same results;

- local (town or village) arrangements to co-ordinate/integrate local services;

- joint information and/or advice centres or 'one stop shops';

- jointly published information about services, local authority activities, etc.;

- provision of information about local services and initiatives to members at the other level(s);

- co-option or invitation to join debate or discussion on matters of local interest;

- joint co-operation with other services and providers (e.g. NHS).

Co-operation between tiers of local government is, of course, only part of the story. Governance at the most local level will bring into play co-operation and collaboration between other agencies and providers.

Where there is more than one tier of local government, counties and districts will need to sort out roles in relation to local governance. Their respective responsibilities will often dictate this but the issue needs to be confronted openly — not least so there is understanding among the other participants in the process. Where there is now a hybrid pattern and a unitary council adjacent to (or surrounded by) a county and its districts there will need to be the same discussion and clarity.

❑ Different kinds of community and (local) civil society

It is easy, and natural, for local government to think in spatial terms particularly when talking about ways of getting closer to people. Place is obviously important as local authorities are geographically entities; councillors represent defined areas; and people live and work in places and easily relate to them. But contemporary society is more complicated than that. For most of us there are other communities which are as important, or more important, than place. We are part of communities of *interest* — communities of gender, race, religion, leisure interest, charitable object, and so on. These committees open other opportunities for local government which we easily lose sight of. If local government is genuinely interested in meeting people where they are, understanding what society is looking to government for, seeing its organisations from the outside in and seeking to involve and empower, then these may be as important as communities of place.

At a recent seminar an Anglican bishop revealingly made the point in relation to a set of rural villages. Using a map which showed clearly communities of place, he overlaid it with slides of other kinds of community — the farming interest, school involvement, sporting affiliations, church membership, the WI, health interest and an HIV group. Suddenly the traditional map was replaced by a series of networks connecting people across spatial boundaries and linking them to surrounding towns and villages. This is a different set of affiliations and a different reality: different kinds of community and, of course, the possibilities for different kinds of conflict. The question is how to relate to them.

The emergence of the new democracies of East and Central Europe has underlined the importance of such affiliations in another way. The old communist regimes had ensured there were no (or as few as possible) intermediate institutions, obstructing the supremacy and control of the state. The new democracies find themselves with few voluntary associations and interest groups. They are encouraging their growth, both as a proper manifestation of a plural society and also as a means of anchoring the individual citizen in the nation state. We have a flourishing civil society — a rich tapestry of communities of interest (some well organised, some less so) — but local government has yet to make as strong connections between civil society and its governance as it might.

This is another challenge for local government and local governance. Local civil society, by its nature, must not become the creature of the (local) state and its governance, but it does offer possibility of highly productive interaction if only it can be got right. Most councils, of course, do have relationships with a wide range of voluntary and special interest groups. How these relationships are used is another matter. Some organisations are there to do a job and provide (often by contract or formal agreement) a service; others are there with an axe to grind and a role as irritant or pressure group. The question is how far these groups can be used as a link with local society and as a source of local learning or as a channel between the public and its governance. Their strength, incidentally, is often in marked contrast to the relatively weak membership of political parties. They thus embody an involvement and a commitment which is important in its own right as well as one which underpins local society.

As local authorities think the implications of this through, there are three particular issues which present themselves:

- The first is about the way people can be drawn into the political process through such communities, and organisation and public debate enriched in the process. There will be a need to face conflicts between different interests. An eye must be kept open for the grinding of axes, a watchful eye kept on representativeness and every effort made to seek out groups not instinctively prepared to have their say. That is manageable and should not deflect attention from the potential. Groups can be empowered by giving them a voice — either in an 'external' consultative or deliberative process or by bringing them into internal political processes through co-option, membership of working parties and the like. One new unitary council, for example, is engaged in active dialogue with a wide range of voluntary organisations and interest groups both about the shape of its organisation and operations and about major policy issues. Other local authorities have created forums on a range of topics into which groups and organisations are drawn. One county council co-opts representatives of relevant interests on to its main committees. Each of the examples represents a search for new patterns and ways of drawing interests into the process of government.

- The second issue is about seeing such communities as a source of learning. Precisely because they do represent common ground and areas of special interest, they are a means of local government finding out about needs and ways of meeting them. Some of the devices just described lend themselves to this process as well but there are other ways in which rich data can be assembled about what is needed by way of public and other provision, how needs might be met and about the continuing performance of the local authority — and other agencies — in their service delivery and operations. Examples, which are well used, include focus groups, public debates, special meetings and the better flow of information.

- The third issue is about the way in which these same communities can be used as agents in service delivery. There is nothing new in this. Voluntary organisations and the like have played a steadily increasing role in service delivery over the years — sometimes supported with enthusiasm, sometimes with reluctance. Recognising their wider role may give them added weight and legitimacy as agents of service delivery. They have traditionally been seen to have great strengths: better able to personalise services, smaller scale and more flexible in their operations, the ability to innovate and experiment; and, often, bringing an element of competition. At the same time they have sometimes been guilty of amateurism, paternalism, operating according to the whim of their often well to do leaders and dependent on highly unstable funding sources. The ability of local government to bring more reliable funding, public debate about values and priorities and an ability to set and monitor quality standards introduces an important element of balance and the possibility of 'voluntary sector' and 'government' playing to their own strengths.

Contractual relationships have come to underpin this balance in many cases. With them has come the fear that control will undermine the capacity for innovation and experiment and that the cash which underpins this control will be used to extend the dead hand of bureaucracy. Such fears may be misplaced. There is no necessary reason for contracts and financial payments to have this effect. Indeed, a recognition of the wider importance of voluntary groups as a key part of local civil society and representative of its plurality, and the part that they can play as intermediary between government and people, bringing the one closer to the other, may well help.

In short, different ways of looking at 'community' open up an important agenda. For most local authorities there is probably more potential than has yet been realised though there will always be the need to watch for who is not involved.

For local government there is urgent need to tease out new patterns and new relationships between the local authority and the plurality of voluntary and community groups and to exploit the opportunities to draw closer to them and their people. Here, of course, the boundary between local government and local governance quickly becomes blurred. Communities of interest are an intermediary within the wider process of local governance as well as with the local authority. Moreover, in so far as these organisations are playing a part in service provision and delivery and have an interest in the shape and direction of their locality, they are players in the process of local governance.

❏ Closer to service users

We have put the emphasis so far on ways in which local government and governance can be brought closer to the public at large and on ways in which more emphasis can be given to a bottom-up approach as opposed to a top down one. There is another important theme, and that is the way in which local government's services relate to *their* public, those who use them.

For all the attention given to the Citizens' Charter in the last few years, it is worth recalling that it is nine or ten years ago that many local authorities really began to address their relationships with their customers seriously. In the intervening period there cannot be a council which has not tried to improve that relationship and make itself more open and explicitly responsive. That effort has also demonstrated something which is very important. It is exceedingly difficult to keep an organisation genuinely outward looking and customer focused. Initiatives can be taken, but old ways soon seem to creep back. Whatever may be said about service to, for, or with the public being a key part of public management, the evidence certainly points toward the need for continuous renewal. That renewal needs to be about substance. Superficial attempts to improve relationships which do not change attitudes and actual behaviours and performance will only cause frustration and cynicism.

There seems to be a whole series of imperatives in organisational life which get in the way of the external relationships and insulate an organisation from the outside world. The 'we know best' attitudes of professionals and politicians, the pressures of organisational convenience, the desire for uniformity and the dominance of professional ideas and fashions are all good examples. Local government is not peculiar in this. There is extensive research and writing about the private sector which recognises similar problems. It was well publicised and materials published by the Local Government Training Board in the mid 1980s began to draw local government's attention to the issues. They are, in many ways, as relevant today as they were then — even if circumstances and the requirements of the Citizens' Charter have moved the world on.

The starting point has to be, yet again, thinking about the whole organisation and recognising that most facets of its life and existence impact on its relationships with its customers. And, indeed its citizens; in concentrating here on service relationships there is no intention to down play the importance of getting right that wider relationship. Structures (the way in which they impede or facilitate problem solving and service delivery) and processes (the way in which customers are dealt with, decisions made and services provided) together with supporting systems and procedures and people (the way the organisation is and people are, their skills and their facility for handling the public) are all important. None can win the battle alone; the management task is to hold all the strands together and to ensure each is making a positive contribution.

That having been said (and done!) the good service organisation has then to make sure it has particular characteristics in place to facilitate a close relationship. For example, it has to:

- be accessible, physically (its buildings, office, enquiry points, etc.) and psychologically (the way it presents itself in terms of openness, welcome, etc.);

- provide good clear information about itself (its services, what can be expected of them standards, levels of service, etc.) and so on;

- communicate well (clear, understandable language; minimum bureaucratic paperwork) and with people where they are (at home as well as in public spaces, using different media and appropriate languages);

- be able to solve the problems presented with minimum fuss (e.g. manage its relationships with contiguous service providers with as little disruption and as much co-ordination as possible);

■ be clear and explicit when things cannot be done or happen in a
particular way (public services inevitably involve rationing and
rationing needs explanation if it is to be understood).

The catalogue can be extended but the point is made. The question is how
many councils and services can genuinely say that they are beyond reproach.
It is not difficult to do a quick audit (with the help of customers) and establish
what still needs attention, salutary though that can be.

The common experience of many different local authorities draws attention to
five particular issues which are particularly important when customer
relationships are addressed.

Creating a service culture

Whatever the individual parts of a good service organisation, a key part of
holding to the holistic view is to create a culture which is about service and
putting the public first. The ethos of and pride in *public* management should
help in this. It is something of which not enough is made in local government,
even though it is the reason many people work in it. At its heart is a set of:

■ shared understandings about what is important (i.e. service and public)
in the organisation;

■ shared values and beliefs about why that is the case.

Such a culture can be nurtured and fostered by politicians and senior
managers demonstrating its importance through what they say and do and by
the organisation as a whole in what it does. It can be reinforced by the way in
which the local authority works internally. For example it can:

■ ensure that its own staff at the frontline are listened to as a source of
learning about how it is doing;

■ use its own employees — as service users and citizens — as a source of
market research and ideas about improvement;

■ strive to encourage and empower staff to use their customer-centred
discretion and support it;

■ continually underline the seamlessness of the organisation by refusing
to concentrate on any one aspect of service in isolation.

Equally, it can be easily undermined by such things as:

- superficial statements not supported by action;
- giving people discretion to act and then blaming them for their actions;
- closed and exclusive decision making;
- finding out what service users want and then ignoring the information.

While each action may be small on its own, taken together with other similar actions they can continually shape and re-shape (or undermine) a supportive culture. Amongst other things, this will serve as a counter balance to the forces which turn the organisation in on itself, encouraging a pattern of action dictated by its own convenience or a 'we know best' attitude.

Public service and contracting out

It is easy to talk about creating a service culture when the local authority itself is the provider. What happens when provision is contracted out to another organisation — in the public, private or voluntary sectors? It is obviously much more difficult but nevertheless important. Central will be the relationship with the 'contractor'. The more formal, rule bound and regulated that relationship, the more difficult it will be (i.e. contracts resulting from a competitive tendering regime will be particularly problematic). The more open and flexible the relationship (usually entered into voluntarily) the more scope there will be to develop shared understandings about the nature and purpose of the service and the kind of values and approaches which should underlie its public provision.

The point about re-defining the nature of public management, given the multiplicity of organisations now involved in public service provision, needs to be stated and sorted out urgently. Of course other organisations will bring their own sets of values and approaches to management and delivery. What is needed is an attempt to trace out and define the common ground.

Finding out

The point has already been made that part of being close to people is finding out what is needed or expected — and how the organisation is doing in meeting those things. The devices for finding out such as surveys, suggestion schemes, complaints procedures, consultative groups and so on, are well known. What seems to be less well known or to present more of a problem, is how to use the information. Collecting data is all well and good. It is only worthwhile if its product is then built into review and decision making processes. This seems to present difficulties. It is not clear whether it is because the results may be uncomfortable for politicians or professionals; or whether it is that the symbolism of collecting views is all that seems important. Making sure what is found out is then taken into account is essential.

At the heart of 'finding out' is listening to the customer. An increasing number of organisations find that talking to people directly rather than at second hand yields a rich seam of data and help. The Department of Health actually recommended (in 1992) that health authorities create panels to bring members of the parties together to sound out ideas and collect reactions to the way things are done.

It is estimated that around 25 per cent of health authorities have done this. There is no equivalent estimate for local government. What we do know is that user panels, focus groups and the like are used by a growing, even if small, number and that the product has been well worth the investment of time and energy. For example:

- one metropolitan council, has joined with its local health authority to create a statistically representative panel of 1,000 people whom it questions three times a year about needs and services — to great effect;

- another uses a similar arrangement to collect and assess views on budget issues.

Many other councils have used similar approaches for more limited purposes.

Service users as co-producers

One way in which services can come closer to the people, and those using them be empowered, is by recognising that, often, the services can only be effectively used where the user is seen and accepted as a co-producer. Service and servility are well and truly separated. The vulnerable family being supported by the social work team, the library user, the school student (and perhaps her/his family), the planning applicant, the housing tenant are all examples where only co-operative effort will produce effective service.

Important starting points are recognising users as co-producers or partners by:

- helping them use the service effectively and managing them as productive resources who bring a valuable contribution — the 'moment of truth' — to the actual service transaction;

- encouraging service users to give leadership and direction to front line managers (often they are in a more direct relationship than senior managers) and help in determining levels of service (i.e. participant market researchers);

- giving them the opportunity to comment on and review the shape and nature of the organisation and its performance and to contribute to ideas for change.

The idea of the co-producer is part of taking a different view of the public as one who shares in service production not as one who is 'done to' in the delivery of service.

Charters, standards and educating the customer

One of the advances of recent years, associated not least with the Citizens' Charter, has been the greater attention given to defining standards and levels of service and of measuring performance against these definitions. The latter may have given rise to much debate about the utility of league tables, indicators and quantitative measures, but they have undeniably brought benefit. It is right to be cautious about what is being measured and about over-simplification, but that does not deny the importance of searching for good indicators and measures and of using even imperfect tools to compare performance, to question and learn.

The more explicit are the definitions and the standards articulated, the more onus it puts on the educated user who is able to digest and handle the information available. Apart from anything else such users are obviously more likely to be effective co-producers. An increasingly important part of being a good (public) service organisation in the future is going to be finding a way of educating, supporting and helping users of services understand what is provided, how to judge it and make appropriate choices and share in its delivery effectively. Training and information programmes should be available to staff; their equivalent need to be developed for users.

Thus it should be important to both members and managers that **a key part of being closer to the people will be getting right the service relationships. This will involve taking a holistic view of the organisation and its working but it will also involve seeking better ways of creating an appropriate culture, sharing this across other providing agencies, improving techniques of listening and finding out, recognising users as co-producers and educating/supporting users to be more effective.** Important though these service relationships are for local government (and other public services) they obviously need to be set in the broader context of relationships with citizens in general. The latter are not only potential users, they are people to whom the public service is accountable and on whose behalf public provision is made. As ever, there is a balance to be struck and no one relationship ignored.

HOW TO USE THIS CHAPTER

- How good are you and your colleagues at taking a bottom-up view of the local authority and its work? How is it best done?

- What kinds of decentralisation take place in your council? What are the benefits and disadvantages? Is there scope for more? If so, what?

- What happens about local governance at the most local levels? Is it enough? Does it have much substance? What are the possibilities for more?

- How good is the council at recognising communities of interest as well as places? How does it engage with organised groups and societies? Is this a way of strengthening ownership of local government and enriching debate and decisions? What are the next steps?

- Are your services user-centred? How much of what happens is driven by the organisation and its preferences? How do you build a service culture? Is there more scope for seeing users as co-producers?

- Are citizens in general, as well as service users seen as important? How do you get the balance right?

114

8

Commissioning and services

❏ Commissioning

When we come to talk about services and meeting the needs of localities, there are two key considerations. First, and most important, the local authority continues to have major responsibilities. Whether services are actually provided from within the organisation or whether external agencies are contracted to provide, the council retains the ultimate responsibility. This service responsibility tends to be down played in discussions about changes in local government and, in particular, the re-discovery of local governance.

The second consideration relates to that broader local governance. There are other parts to public provision in any locality and there will be needs which will be met by other organisations than the local authority. The local authority, however, is a key player, has a justifiable interest in all aspects of the locality's life and brings to the table the special legitimacy which comes from the democratic process with its possibilities to exercise choice and voice. Shaping of the total provision and defining what needs to be done is therefore a key part of local governance (whether this is organised in a wholly piecemeal or a more systematic and organised way) and so an issue for local government.

The fact of ultimate responsibility for a defined set of services, and the issue of determining what needs to be done in the locality, both point to an important role which has been inadequately played in the past and for which local government certainly does not have an appropriate language.

One of the interesting things about the changes which have arisen from the development of contracting, particularly the emergence of markets and a mixed economy of service provision, has been the split of the purchaser or client from the provider or contractor. We shall return to this later. Suffice it to say here that, whatever the strengths and weaknesses of split, it has put an emphasis on knowing what needs to be provided, on specification and definition and on somebody ensuring it happens in line with those definitions. This is important — not least because these things were not taken seriously enough in the past. However, the language of 'purchaser' or 'client' is too narrow. It places too much emphasis on the act of purchase and on the business of managing some kind of contract or agreement to provide.

Interestingly enough, in the health service, while this language has been used, more attention has been given to the concept of *commissioning*. While this implies 'purchasing' or acting as 'client', and while it may well concern specification and definition as well as managing contractual relationships, it also implies something more. The implication that there has been a set of prior activities: review and assessment of need and judgement of priorities as a result of which there are detailed decisions about levels of provisions and arrangements for delivery. On the face of it, a pedantic point — but with deep implications.

The idea of commissioning links with two other things. It takes us back to our earlier discussion of strategic management. Though distinct, there are some shared characteristics — knowing and understanding what is going on in the external environment, being clear about pressures and trends of change, being selective, making judgements and choices. All of this, conceptually at least, is kept apart from the routine operations of 'doing', with their focus on particular activities, client groups and so on. It is about planning the wood before planting the trees. And it is this which makes a second connection.

A frequently heard public management aphorism is about government's concern with 'steering not rowing'. That, too, puts an emphasis on separating out the business of operations from setting direction and approach. Just as we made the point about the close linkage between the strategic and operational manager, so this distinction can only be taken so far. A key ingredient of the learning needed about the environment and what is happening in it comes from the actual delivering of services and the discharging of other responsibilities. However real the conceptual distinction, the reality needs to provide for close working relationships and the free flow of information between the two sides. The importance of the conceptual distinction is that it does point to a set of important tasks which need to be allowed for and to the need to have structures, processes and people capable of seeing them through.

Whether we are talking about the specific responsibilities of local government or the interests of the wider local governance it is important that:

- steps are taken to find out and assess what the needs of the locality are;

- judgements are made about relative priority between the needs defined; and

- careful attention given to different ways in which needs can be met and the range and variety of people and organisations who might play a part before detailed decisions are taken which set the shape, level and operational pattern of service.

These early stages, through to the point of setting and overseeing the arrangements for implementation, are what commissioning is about. Before moving on to look at particular parts of the commissioning role, there are some detailed points worth noting about its components:

- In Chapter 7 we emphasised the importance of 'finding out' and listening to customers and of being close to people. Identifying needs and establishing what requires to be done in the locality involves close interaction between local government and its communities: fact finding and information gathering, discussion and debate.

- Local governance puts a proper emphasis on the whole locality and the totality of its public provision. This underlines the need for ways of bringing all the agencies and organisations involved into debate and discussion. As we said in Chapter 4, this is unlikely to happen spontaneously. Some kind of formal structure and process, however lightly applied, is probably necessary. The local authority is in a key position to lead and influence the process. Its own political processes will obviously be used to make judgements and choices about the things under its control. They can bring legitimacy and support to the wider debate.

- Complicated as it may seem, the processes are more likely to be iterative and continuing than once and for all or even fitting a regular planning cycle.

- The commissioning process carries implications, too, for the kind of people involved. There needs to be a blend of strategic and general management skills, with a new kind of professional input capable of concentrating on overall need and provision rather than the detail of delivery and cases. The people concerned will need to operate in an open way and in close association with other organisations and the public at large.

■ Decisions about how problems should be tackled and by whom will require careful analysis and debate and need to be free of bias. Often answers may seem obvious because of convention and tradition (for example, assumptions about self-sufficiency and direct delivery and conventional patterns still run deep in local government and are shared in other organisations). There is one reason for discussing the issues further below.

What is important, taking account of these individual issues is that **the idea of commissioning is taken seriously and that organisational arrangements are made to support assessment of the locality's needs, priority and choice, decisions about how best to meet them and oversight of implementation.**

❑ Deciding 'how'

For a local authority to think only about its own provision and to assume that a self-sufficient approach is the right one greatly simplifies matters. In this case, to do something new or different just means adapting the organisation and getting on with it. The challenge to the idea of the self-sufficient local authority and a renewed emphasis on the multiplicity of alternative providers has opened up a whole new set of possibilities and problems. Of course, there never was uniform self-sufficiency: private contractors supplied goods and built roads and buildings; voluntary organisations made all kinds of contribution, particularly in the social care field, and so on. That is not the point. What is, is that there is a growing willingness to take nothing for granted and to carefully think through what the possibilities are; and then, having done this, to make informed judgement about what is best — even if some councils instinctively prefer 'in-house' solution and others look to private contractors.

But there is even more than this. It is not just a question of 'who'? but of 'how'? The range of policy tools or instruments — alternative means of service delivery — is wide and we return to them below. An important part of the commissioning is to work through the possibilities and choose the right mix. Although this kind of analysis always happened in some fields, it is a stage in the process which has received too little attention. There is now a chance to change the balance.

However there are important issues which go to the heart of democratic government and traditional public management which need to be recognised. They include issues about:

- Accountability, because implementation may well involve people who are only indirectly accountable to local politicians.

- Traditional approaches to management, which have been concerned with hands-on control and exercising direct authority. Many of the people now involved in a contractual relationship will be employees of other organisations and often not in the public sector at all. This points to two things. First new skills, approaches and techniques will need to be used by the local authority in its management task. Secondly, it brings us back to the issue of how we define *public* management and where the boundaries really are.

- Co-ordination and the role of the commissioning local authority in orchestrating numbers of different players, interests and activities. As we saw in Chapter 5, the integrating capacity of the local authority needs to grow considerably.

The last point again takes us back to the broader arena of local governance. Each of the issues which faces the local authority has a relevance for the whole.

The explicit recognition of the range of policy tools and instruments available to the local public policy-maker is further advanced in the United States than anywhere else. The International City Management Association generated an important debate in the late 1980s and produced well used guidance about how to analyse and select 'appropriate' means of service delivery. That debate was probably inhibited in the UK by the all-consuming need to implement CCT. It is paradoxical that a central government tool designed to create an alternative model — and which did so much to break the conventional mind-set — should have itself inhibited a broader search by substituting one simple mode of action for another.

More recently the book by Osborne and Gaebler, *Re-inventing Government*, pulled together a wide range of 'alternatives'. They culled these from an examination of developing local practice across the US. Some of their list of 36 categories are very much specific to the American context but most will be recognisable to a British audience. They are a mix of harder and softer, direct and indirect devices and include such things as:

- grants,

- subsidies,

- loans,

- contracts,

- franchises,

- partnerships (with other public, private and voluntary organisations),

- regulation,

- licensing,

- technical assistance and information provision (to potential providers),

- volunteers and voluntary organisations,

- vouchers,

- self-help,

- co-production,

- market management.

In the UK, a not dissimilar list — though more restricted — has come from work by the Plunkett Foundation funded by the DTI. (See *Ownership for Local Authority Services: A Guide for Policy-makers* (1993) by the Plunkett Foundation Long Hanborough.)

The wider the selection of options the more important the business of choosing becomes. Again, American research and practice has probably gone furthest. From this comes a list of criteria against which alternatives can be judged:

- the extent to which services can be specified and defined;

- how many producers (or potential producers) there are and whether there is real competition;

- the efficiency and effectiveness of any arrangements;

- the scale of the service or task and thus the size of organisation needed;

- the extent to which there is direct payment for the service received;

- responsiveness to service users;

- susceptibility to fraud;

- the extent to which equity matters;

- responsiveness to government direction.

So far as providers are concerned, they may be in the public, private or voluntary sectors (or some combination). The point was made in Chapter 7 that there are inevitably strengths and weaknesses in the characteristics of each. Part of the decision about how to deliver a particular service or responsibility will be to balance these. The Osborne and Gaebler work is again instructive — and transferable to the UK. They argue that the **public** sector is best at:

- policy management;
- regulation;
- ensuring equity;
- preventing discrimination or exploitation;
- continuity and stability;
- being concerned for social cohesion.

whereas it is less good at flexibility, rapid change, responsiveness and customisation of provision — even though it may try hard.

The **private** sector is in many respects the reverse of this, being good at these last things and at investment and replicating successful innovation (and so enhancing profits). It is less good at policy management, equity, continuity and preventing discrimination and building cohesion. The profit motive is good at driving some things but averse to others!

The **voluntary** sector, on the other hand, is best at tasks which:

- generate little or no profit margin;
- require compassion and commitment;
- require a holistic approach to problems;
- require trust on the part of customers;
- require hands-on personal attention;
- benefit from experiment and small-scale innovation.

The voluntary sector usually brings a strong set of (moral) values and is good at encouraging individual responsibility. On the other hand, as we pointed out in the last chapter, it can easily exhibit paternalism and be selective in the interests it serves. It also has difficulty in generating large-scale resources.

Careful analysis of a situation, particular problems to be dealt with, constraints to be recognised or tasks to be performed will usually quickly reduce the range of options. **What is important, for elected members as well as the managers concerned in the commissioning process, is that decisions about appropriate policy tools and instruments are approached with as open a mind as possible and decisions made with careful assessment of the options, against clear criteria and a weighing of the relative costs and benefits.** There will seldom be only one way of doing something: usually there will be a range of possibilities. Prior assumptions about what is best may, at best, be misleading; at worst they will undermine the successful and effective implementation of policy. Equally, emphasis on the good management of implementation should not be allowed to 'crowd out' what the best means of implementation is. The content of policy and the tools or instruments used will both have the major impact on the solving of policy problems.

❏ Contracts and contracting

A number of the tools available will involve contracting in one form or another. As we saw in Chapter 4 contracting has become a significant feature of the local government management landscape in recent years as a result of CCT, LMS and their generation of a contract culture. There are some specific points to be made about them.

It may be that the worst excesses are past, but there was a point at which no relationship seemed sound unless it was underpinned by a contract (and all the better if that contract had been competitively won or, at least, the market tested along the way). Contracts have their place, but need to be approached with open eyes. On the one hand they involve costs (not least the transaction costs involved in their operation and management) as well as benefits and run the danger of creating their own bureaucracy; on the other, there is a danger that they are seen in an over-simplified way. Looked at from a quite different perspective, some people may see them as inextricably tied up with government policy and the world of CCT in particular thus to be eschewed if at all possible.

Commissioning a service or activity via a contract requires definition of what is to be provided, requires explicit statement of this and provision for appropriate monitoring and review. It also should mean that the contractor (in-house or external) is the organisation best able to demonstrate the right balance of effectiveness, efficiency and economy. Such a process is likely to be seen as benefits. The problem is that to establish a contract (particularly if it is via competitive process), and to manage and monitor/review it, entails costs and runs the risk of building a dedicated bureaucracy along the way. Some of the studies of CCT, for example, have shown that savings have been significantly reduced by the transaction costs involved. Assuming there is freedom to decide what to do, it is important to be as rigorous as possible in undertaking analysis of costs and benefits.

As a general rule of thumb, transaction costs will be high:

- when the contracting process is hedged in by detailed regulation and requirements (as in CCT);

- where the tasks being contracted are difficult or complicated and where they vary greatly;

- where monitoring and evaluation are difficult to undertake or complex in nature;

- where there is a high level of uncertainty.

Transaction costs will also depend on the nature of the contract and on the kinds of relationships which result. Contracts tend to be most obviously thought of in classic form: a long term, legal agreement containing detailed provision for the dealings between the parties involved as time unfolds. For local government this would mean a specification of the service to be provided under different sets of circumstances, a definition of the time the agreement is to run and how it will be monitored and reviewed. To limit thinking to this, however, is to over-simplify. There are other kinds of contract. Most obviously, there is the 'spot' contract which is very much part of day to day life for most people and organisations. An immediate and on the spot agreement is made to transact a particular exchange. It takes place quickly and with minimal transaction cost; whether or not it is repeated is irrelevant; it is simple — and probably not thought of as a contract at all.

More important is the kind of contract which is about continuing and long term relationships, but which lacks the explicit and detailed provisions of the classic contract. That is to say, it relies heavily on implicit undertakings and involves a high degree of trust, with the parties involved having expectations of one another which go way beyond the terms of the contract. An employment contract is a good example; here there is a formal contract as a base but a relationship — and a set of expectations — which go way beyond its explicit provisions. Such contracts are appropriate where flexibility is required and benefit is to be gained from the free exchange of information (in contrast, a classic contract can inhibit flexible response and the flow of information).

Those 'relational' contracts are likely to work only where the contracting parties are of roughly equal strength and where there is mutual interest in forming and making a success of a continuing relationship. It is of course simple to break a contract based as much on trust as on law and doing so may often carry short term gains. They are thus much less common in the marketplace than classic contracts (and, of course, 'spot' contracts). Their disadvantage is that they can carry scope for corruption.

What do we take from these distinctions? First, that CCT and the drivers of the contract culture have tended to see the contract in classic terms. Secondly, classic contracts are more suitable for some circumstances than others. Where there is low risk, minimal uncertainty and thus the possibility of specifying in precise terms what is required, without the subsequent need to adapt and modify, this kind of contract serves its purpose well. Refuse collection, street cleaning, grounds maintenance (notwithstanding the vagaries of climate) are good examples. The greater the complexity and the higher the risks and the uncertainties and thus the need for flexibility, the more difficult it will be to create the kind of framework within which the classic contract makes sense. Social care and professional services make the point.

And so, thirdly, in circumstances of uncertainty and complexity, contracts which place high value on relationships and levels of trust between the parties and of evolutionary development over the longer term are better suited. The difficulty is that they are not easy to create, certainty cannot be established immediately, and they do not meet the kind of regulatory requirements demanded by a compulsory regime. The question which needs to be pursued is how far they can be used and how they are best developed — to gain the benefit of contracting in general, while avoiding the impediments of the classic contract. Put another way, while it may be necessary to begin a contractual relationship via a classic model, as the relationship develops and trust is built, how far can the explicit be allowed to become implicit and flexibility replace rigidity?

The contract is a convenient basis for an arms length relationship and for managing it. It will thus have a critical part to play in many of the policy instruments and tools — alternative means of service delivery — which are available. **It is essential, however, that the appropriateness of contracting, its costs as well as its benefits, and the best form of contractual relationship are carefully thought through. The possibilities for building continuing long term relationships based on mutuality and trust and capable of flexibility and adaptability should be pushed as far as they can.**

There is another aspect of the contract and the commissioner/client/ purchaser – contractor split worth noting too. The conceptual benefits must not be allowed to develop into a reality in which effective operations are undermined. We have made the point that the classical contract may inhibit the free flow of information (not least because its use by one party may damage the other). Yet we have also emphasised the importance of frontline staff as key elements in the processes of learning and finding out. Constructing institutional arrangements which cause the split to become a divide (or turn the Chinese wall into a brick wall) and which prevent that flow of learning will almost certainly harm effectiveness. Instead arrangements need to be made for the transfer of information, exchange of staff to develop shared understanding and to construct a relationship which can identify and exploit common interests. Policy and implementation may be two sides of a coin but they are the same coin and are inextricably linked.

❏ Making the best use of resources

Part of the commissioner's responsibility, however services are ultimately provided and by whatever means, will be to make sure that available resources are put to the best possible use. Traditional value for money concerns should thus be high on the agenda. Two particular considerations are worth noting here, both of which relate to issues already discussed. First of all there is an issue about the scale of public expenditure and what it is used for. Secondly, there are issues about performance review.

It is a reasonable assumption that, for the foreseeable future, the downward pressure on public spending will continue. There is little evidence to suggest anyone has much stomach for major rises in taxation and public spending increases. That means the pressure will be on:

- to exploit whatever alternative sources of funding are available (European funds, the lottery, partnership funding and private finance), and

- to make sure both that the balance of spending is right in terms of local priorities and that spending is being used to maximum effect.

While the former undoubtedly requires imagination and persistence it is relatively straightforward. The latter, for both elected members and managers, is much more difficult. Matching resources to priorities means first being clear about priorities — while competing claims are most conveniently met with a degree of ambiguity. It then means taking a rigorous approach to budgeting, being prepared to challenge traditional patterns and vested interests, and to have the will to follow through the consequences. In the real, as opposed to the theoretical, world there will always be compromises. The question is how many local authorities are persistent enough in following the principles.

There is a second, related issue. It is not just a question of getting the balance of spending right between the various priorities, there is also the question of how the money is spent within services. Despite the VFM rhetoric and the protestations of economy and efficiency from local authorities, there must be a big question about how far local authorities have really gone in the quest to ensure maximum resources for public service delivery. If there is no — or little — new money available, this quest will become all-important.

The work of the Audit Commission has been important in suggesting ways in which resources can be best used and in encouraging good practice; for example the 1994 *People, Pay and Performance* report and its suggestion of significant savings being possible from resources consumed in unnecessary central overheads and poor deployment of staff. The £500 million figure in the report put local government on the defensive and led to allegations about it being impossible to substantiate and so on. The study's subsequent audit will prove the point one way or another but the signs are of under-estimation not exaggeration.

If we strip away the froth of controversy there is an important issue to be addressed. There is a range of evidence to suggest that **public organisations are inclined to 'thicken' not 'thin' and that the culture of local government has made it particularly difficult to take a rigorous and radical look at white collar and professional jobs and what staff do. This will have to change — uncomfortable though it may be — if councils and their public are to be assured that scarce resources are being deployed to maximum effect.**

That inevitably draws attention to performance review. The growing importance of contracting and the influence of the Citizens' Charter movement on making service standards and the like more explicit are two things which have given renewed impetus to monitoring and review. While both may be more difficult than some would have us believe, both are important parts of good management and of ensuring an effective organisation. Four important points are worth making:

■ Re-iterating the argument in Chapter 7 that review of services should involve both front-line staff and service users as both of whom have an important perspective on the way the organisation operates and services are delivered.

- Their evidence will be primarily qualitative but that does not make it any more or less valuable. The absence of figures should not be reason to discount it.

- The comparative data which comes from the Audit Commission and others about the performance of other organisations has a vital part to play — not so much in pointing to firm conclusions as in suggesting where questions need to be asked and to clues about evidence and information which should be sought.

- Bench-marking, in the sense of setting standards and looking to comparators, also provides a useful input to review — again more in raising questions than in providing evaluative judgements.

Performance review should be as important to elected members in their oversight of the organisation and stewardship of its resources as it should be to managers in their task of seeing that the organisation is performing effectively, with due regard to economy and efficiency. For both, though, there has often been less preparedness to ask difficult questions and to see the conclusions of review become part of the continuing operational processes than there should have been. Reviewing and responding to what is discovered in review is part of being a learning organisation.

❏ Service design, rationing, quality and equality

Finding out, assessing need, making choices of priority, selecting delivery mechanisms and review are still only part of the commissioning of services. Service design is another important stage along the way — shaping and planning the way in which services are delivered and the end users treated. Design considerations obviously take us back to the last chapter. For example to:

- close relationships with service users;

- the development of a service culture;

- the encouragement of the concept of co-production.

But there are other issues. Taken together they demonstrate that service design is multi-faceted. While they are important for any local authority, like much of the agenda they will be particularly crucial for the newly created unitary authorities where there is the rare opportunity to more or less start from scratch.

Four issues of current importance serve to illustrate the point. First, a negative one. Resources are finite and often outstripped by demand. **Rationing** is thus a common feature of the public services. Paradoxically, it is at its most difficult where there is a good service, well presented and delivered, which encourages further demand but where there are no additional resources to call upon. Whereas in the private sector demand can be encouraged, producing more resources to create a larger supply to match, this cannot happen in the public sector where there is likely to be no financial exchange involved. Designing services thus has to be, in part, about their allocation. There may be a deliberate decision to favour some individuals or groups over others.

Being clear about the criteria and being prepared to be explicit about them and their application will be important. Without this there is certain to be irritation, frustration, anger and even alienation.

Decisions about the criteria and the nature of allocation will be political ones whereas the act of rationing is likely to be a managerial one. In order to avoid arbitrary decisions or the use of informal customs and practices, both members and officers have to play a part — and accept each other's part.

The second issue is about **quality**. Another of the 'buzz words' of modern management but one of enormous importance. Public expectations, and the possibilities of public providers, both point in the same direction and quality is on the agenda of all local authorities. As ever there is a distinction between rhetoric and reality. Quality should be basic to service design, but the point to be made here is that it needs careful definition (beyond a feeling that 'you know it when you meet it'). It needs the identification of criteria and standards and there needs to be agreement on how it is assessed — involving users as well as 'producers'. To track it without rigour and systems will raise expectations and almost certainly produce frustration.

The third issue is about **equity and equality** — that is, about evenness of access and ensuring there is no discrimination inherently built into service provision. Their importance has grown as it has become recognised that there are all sorts of ways in which discriminatory practice creeps in. It is important that any such issues are explicitly confronted in service design. In particular

- access to service and the need to ensure that language, time, cultural conventions and traditions and the like do not serve to put some groups or individuals at a disadvantage;

- the way in which the user is treated by staff and the need to make sure that personal attitudes, unacceptable behaviour or, simply, misplaced assumptions do not exclude anyone;

- possible mis-use of the service as a result of wrong information, misunderstanding or misplaced expectation which may, again, serve to discriminate against particular individuals or groups (and the categories are wide ranging — most obviously, race, gender and religion; but also, potentially, the young, old, handicapped, single parents, unemployed, etc.);

- the outcome of service transactions involving particular groups or individuals who may be disadvantaged — allocation of school places to children of ethic minority families; use of 'sink' housing estates for allocating houses to 'troublesome' tenants; and so on.

It is too easy to believe that these things just do not happen or will sort themselves out. Discrimination may result from conscious action by staff or it may be unconscious or unintended. It is essential to put appropriate procedures, training and monitoring into place — and to try and think through how the organisation and service ought to be if there are to be no disenfranchised service users. This is likely to involve close exchange with the individuals or groups most likely to be affected.

The fourth point is different again but brings together aspects of quality and equality. It is about **complaints** procedures and the provisions for **redress**. This is another facet of service delivery which has been highlighted by the Citizens' Charter initiatives and one where there is continuing evidence of local government's poor performance. The danger is that the organisation regard complaints as negative, little is seen to happen and the user is left frustrated by the experience. Taking a positive view of complaints is part of developing a strong service and customer-centred culture. It also involves:

- taking seriously 'exit' arrangements so that those who have been in touch with the council and services leave the experience feeling good about it;

- being explicit about what steps to take if the experience has not been good and a complaint is warranted;

- making sure that the steps are easy to take and that the user is helped rather than hindered in doing so;

- having clearly defined response times during which the complainant has an acknowledgement and an explanation of what is happening;

- providing a full explanation at the end of the investigation, an apology if a mistake has been made and an indication of what steps will be taken to prevent recurrence (saying sorry can have a powerful effect by itself, yet public organisations find it difficult);

- developing attitudes which not only take complaints seriously but see them as a useful source of learning for the organisation.

The issue of redress is a more complicated one and susceptible to the '£1 voucher back' syndrome. Forms of redress will not always be appropriate but the possibilities need to be thought through and arrangements made wherever possible. Some kind of redress (even if it is only a repeat of the service transaction that went wrong) often is possible. Together with an apology, it may serve not only to put the matter right but to create loyalty and warm support for the local authority.

Service design is extraordinarily complex and involves many different things. **A key part of service commissioning is a concern for getting the design right, whoever is then involved in delivering it. It obviously implies a close relationship between commissioner and provider — and should thus be of as much interest to elected members as to managers.** It also demands the ability to hold the various facets of service together and to take a holistic view. In a real sense a service is greater than the sum of its parts. And the same is true, of course, of any service in the local public domain. The local authority, as commissioner, is in a position to demonstrate good practice. The other agencies and organisations involved need to demonstrate the same characteristics.

❑ Change by trial, error and success

Services have to be constantly shaped and re-shaped as they respond to a changing environment. New ideas and developments will prompt change. Commissioning and delivering services is thus as much or more about change than stability. The management of that change will raise the kind of issues mentioned in Chapter 6. However, there is an additional point to be made. There are few certainties and there is often a real problem in determining whether a particular initiative or change will be worthwhile, right for its circumstances, realise the anticipated outcomes or have a set of unforeseen consequences. One way of trying to evaluate the worth and impact of proposed changes is to mount pilot ventures or experiments and to monitor carefully what happens before making a final judgement. The willingness to experiment and to learn from the evaluation of success and failure is a hallmark of a learning organisation. It is too easy to assume that uniformity is always the best way of doing things. Acceptance of diversity — and learning from it — is important.

The last decade and more has seen a propensity to go for comprehensive full scale change in public policy and to eschew the opportunities of testing the ideas first — often for fear of losing time or momentum. This has been particularly characteristic of national government initiatives but in many cases (the national curriculum, community care, CCT) local government has been drawn into the process and, as a result, has itself tended to downplay the opportunities for experiment. This is regrettable and the signs of a return to experimentation are to be encouraged. It is not just that it is often difficult to foresee the consequences of policy and changed practice: it is that, all along the way, actual people using services will be involved and affected. **Good management practice should embrace a willingness to pilot, experiment and test new ideas and approaches in service design and delivery to ensure that when change is made it is as well grounded as possible.**

HOW TO USE THIS CHAPTER

- Does the idea of 'commissioning' fit with the way things are done in your authority? How good are you and your colleagues at taking stock of needs, seeing priorities are assessed and then thinking through provisions without prior assumptions?

- What is the range of policy tools and instruments used in your service and area of interest? Is enough thought given to what is best? What alternatives need exploring?

- Do contracts help or get in the way in your activity? Are they the right kind of contract producing the right kind of relationships? Is there trust and confidence?

- Are resources used to the best effect? What about overheads? Is there scope for shifting the balance in favour of service provision? How is this best approached?

- Are the criteria against which your services are decided explicit, understandable and fairly applied? Does enough effort go into explanation? How do you prevent discrimination? Are systems for complaint and redress user-friendly?

9

People

KEY POINTS

- Organisation and people.

- Flexibility, pressures and change.

- Boundary spanning.

- New career patterns.

- Management training and development.

- Organisational development.

- Elected members.

- Developing a learning culture.

- Public management and public service.

A visitor from Australia expressed surprise that in the British local authorities he had visited he had heard 'people are our most important asset' as a repeated refrain. 'Did they really believe and act on this?' he asked. How did it square with down-sizing, increasing pressures and workloads and the like? In Australia, he said, where the public sector is also undergoing enormous change, local authorities were not inclined to place much emphasis on people as people and a key asset. The pressure and pace of change was such that staff were regarded as no more than a convenience (or inconvenience) to be directed, used, or got rid of as necessity dictated.

Making no comment on the Australian situation — and there was probably some exaggeration to make a point — the comments indicate some important dilemmas and issues. UK local government does take its people fairly seriously and some local authorities have track records in people management which compare well with any sector of the economy. Whether people are actually seen as the key asset and treated accordingly is an open question. However one looks at the work of local government — and, for that

132

matter, the wider arena of local governance — people are obviously vital. The way in which people, elected members, managers and all those involved in the delivery of local public services, perform will have a profound impact on the locality. The changes which were noted in Chapter 2, and whose impact has been the recurrent theme of this book, have all manner of people implications. We have hinted at some of them and addressed others. We now need to collect these and add some specific items to our agenda.

❑ Organisation and people

The point has been made that it is essential that an organisation, first, has an agreed and understood purpose and sense of strategic direction. No one can act effectively in a vacuum or in some kind of conceptual, detached way. The content or substance of what it is doing is intrinsic to it. Organisation, however good, can never be a substitute for policy audits and content. Thus, in a real sense, the organisation *per se* is a secondary consideration.

However, we have also said that organisation matters. That is to say, structures, processes *and* people do count. They are the vehicle through which purpose is achieved. To be effective, they must match capacity to what it is that they are trying to do. To have structures which get in the way, processes which inhibit and people who lack the right skills or have the wrong attitudes and approach is a sure way to failure. To have the opposite is to put an organisation at least on the way to success.

A 1980s Tower Hamlets or 1990s South Somerset approach to decentralisation has very different requirements to the traditional, centralised hierarchy which has characterised so much of local government. An authority in pursuit of a highly commercial approach (a Berkshire or a Brent, for example) will be quite different to one which wants to retain a more conventional approach. Patterns and needs will vary from council to council. The signs are that there is a greater willingness to work out what these are case by case. For all of that, we still seem to have some ambivalence about how we perceive the local authority as an organisation. It is a piece of machinery, dedicated to a particular end but capable, as it were, of mechanical adjustment and susceptible to mechanistic interventions and the use of sanctions and rewards? Or is it rather more organic, with a life of its own needing careful nurture and sensitive handling?

Organisation theory pulls us in both directions and management practice often seems to draw from both poles at the same time (PRP, job evaluation, management reviews on the one hand; fascination with culture, organisation development, team building and the like on the other). We often seem not to be sure whether people are cogs in the machine, the impersonal components of traditional bureaucracy, or something much more subtle and sophisticated. The fact of the matter, of course, is that both approaches are helpful in gaining understanding.

This book has inclined towards the organic rather than the mechanistic. To take the argument further, **it may be helpful to visualise the organisation of the local authority as a community, with members rather than employees.** The basis of membership, for most, may be an employment contract but note that as seen in the last chapter, such a contract can be seen as an archetypal 'relational' contract where there is mutual investment, high expectation of one another and a foundation of trust. The idea of organisation as community serves to emphasise a number of things:

- the intangibles (values, belief, etc.) which help hold the organisation together but which can divide them;

- the need which communities have to develop, grow and change;

- hence the importance of investment in training and development;

- a sense of mutuality and of shared responsibility for collective destiny;

- continuity and long term existence and so the importance of thinking about and investing in the future;

- the underlying sense of security which this brings (notwithstanding the impact of unforseen or unavailable short term change);

- the importance of doing more of the same, only better, as a motivating force as well as exploring ways of doing things differently;

- and the commitment which comes from simply being a member of the community.

The analogy may not be wholly satisfactory but it is useful. It points to two other things. First, to where elected members fit in. Councillors can helpfully be thought of as part of the community, albeit with particular responsibilities for directing it or as of it, but perhaps a little apart from it. Their membership, however, gives them common interests with the rest of the community and a willingness to be explicit about differences. They are more than the drivers of a bureaucratic machine — the relationships are more subtle than that.

Secondly, and following from this, there are pointers to a possible re-definition of the officer–member relationship. There is no escaping the formal accountability of the one to the other and the over-arching responsibility of the elected members. However, the idea of community suggests a mutuality and common partnership. To this the officer brings particular information, expertise and experience, just as the councillor brings distinctive responsibilities, skills and experience. The contribution and the partnership need to be respected for what they are. The officer dismissive of the councillor, or the councillor determined to act without regard to the officer is denying collective responsibility.

❏ Flexibility, pressure and change

The Australian visitor also drew attention to the pressures on staff as a result of public sector change. Such comments have been repeated so often they begin to sound trite or like special pleading. They are neither. The pressures — and consequences — of change are real. Local government may share much in common with organisations in other sectors, but it has its own version of change.

Traditional local government has been built on stability, with clearly defined jobs and administrative and managerial tasks, and on finding the best people to fill them. For large numbers of jobs, and particularly managerial ones, that is no longer good enough. Seeking the best people remains important — but what kind of person is best has changed, because the nature of the jobs and work has changed. People will have to be more flexible in their approach and quicker to learn. They will have to become more used to and adept at spanning and working across organisational boundaries. Stable and certain structures will be replaced by flexibility and uncertainty in which the intangibles (values, beliefs, principles) will become increasingly important as the glue which binds the whole. As a consequence of all of this, there is need to have a greater investment in people and in their development.

Some will thrive on the challenges which all this throws up; others will find it difficult. Few will escape the pressures which are associated with change. More insecurity, more work, but fewer people, longer hours, increased complexity, conflicting demands and pressures make a familiar litany. At the heart of thinking about the people issues are the twin needs of finding ways of supporting and helping them to adapt to the new situation and grow, and ensuring that the organisation has, in its people, a resource capable of delivering effectively. **The new management of local government (and other local institutions for that matter) needs to be quicker to adapt to change and better equipped to deal with the fast moving world which confronts it.**

❑ Boundary spanning

A repeated theme of this book — and one of the striking changes just referred to — has been the need to work across organisational boundaries. It has arisen in four different contexts. Firstly, increased differentiation (and, sometimes, fragmentation) inside the local authority, requiring people to work across boundaries. Secondly, the need to make lateral connections in policy development and in operational practice to ensure that problems are addressed and solved as 'wholes', and not divided into arbitrary and artificial parts in housing and social work, social care and the NHS, education and training and so on. This need has become all the more important with the growing significance of the 'wicked' issues (public safety, urban or rural regeneration, the environment, etc.) which have no regard for conventional boundaries within or between organisations.

Thirdly, there are the boundary issues thrown up by the mixed economy of provision and the management of contracts with third parties in the public, private and voluntary sectors. Lastly, it has arisen from the new importance of the wider processes of local governance; from the fact of external differentiation, with the increased number of actors/agencies involved in government at the local level; and from the requirement and willingness to develop joint working in the interests of the locality.

Working and staying within a bounded organisation is relatively easy: there is a degree of certainty and stability, at least in terms of people, relationships, ways of working, culture, environment, and so on. Working across boundaries removes or reduces these certainties. Managing within boundaries is nearer to having direct control of the situation. Managing across boundaries is indirect and requires different skills and qualities. It requires understanding the nature and approach of the other party/parties and it means searching for common ground and values rather than just assuming them to be there. **Procedures and processes need to be put into place to facilitate boundary spanning, with people and their skills being crucial.**

Organisational incentives need to be offered to encourage people to reach out across boundaries, and to exploit the opportunities for doing so as well as for helping ordinary citizens find their way through the organisational maze. Training and development needs to be used to encourage skills in, for example:

- networking

- influencing

- negotiating

- advocacy

- contract management

and to provide an understanding of the way other organisations work and the assumptions on which they are built.

At the same time the conventional approach to management as production, dominant in much of local government, needs to be re-framed — or at least added to by another perspective. The convention has been to determine what has to be done, decide the best way of doing it, apply the resources and judge the results. In the reality of inter-organisational working in local governance, the goals will often only emerge along the way. The driving force may simply be the desire to work together. People need to understand how to work in this fluid and often perverse context. The most striking examples are local partnerships, where often forming the partnership is the first and most important objective; finding something to do then follows later!

Of course, citizens also need to be encouraged to participate. Such things as:

- focus groups

- panels

- neighbourhood or local forums

- public meetings and debate

- involvement in problem solving and service delivery

are all possibilities to be explored — but always on the public's and not the organisation's terms. Working to define what needs to be done, structuring how it is done and helping in the doing are key ways of building public trust, support and confidence in the system of government. A part of boundary spanning is thus about creating processes which involve citizens and help them to participate. Again, the right skills and style will be at a premium. The traditional bureaucrat will be uneasy and unlikely to be successful! Approaches need to be learned and developed.

❏ New career patterns

It would be surprising, given the other changes taking place, if new career paths were not beginning to open up. This is happening, though progress is slow. An important part of renewing local public management should be to have in place people who are good at meeting the new demands and pressures as they meet the purpose and direction of their organisation. Training and development will play an important part (and we shall come to this next) but different career paths which enable new connections to be made, new perspectives formed and broader experience gained could be even more important.

Traditionally, local government has left career planning and career movement largely to the individual. Sometimes there is advice, counsel and encouragement, but seldom more. This needs to change. The limited career paths of today, bounded by profession, service, and function, need to be replaced by wider choice. **A more conscious and systematic approach is needed to provide broader experience. New patterns need to be developed and new opportunities within organisations and outside need to be created and taken.**

What are the requirements? A number have been referred to explicitly, others are implied by the discussion. Taken together, the most important are:

- **General management** — while management needs to be related to the particular content and circumstances of whatever is being managed, there is a still a tendency to rely too heavily on professionals who have moved into managing in their own discipline or service and then stayed there. Because of the importance of managing services day by day, there has also been heavy emphasis on operational management and on direct control. There is a need to encourage more managers to develop a round, corporate perspective and a strategic capacity in approach and thinking and to have experience of managing indirectly across boundaries and through contracts. Managers also need as wide an experience of different settings and circumstances as possible. Taken together, these things are best thought of as general management as compared to service specific management.

- **Lateral working** — The importance of making lateral connections in developing policy and in operations requires managers who think instinctively outside their service department or organisation and are good at making connections. This is further reinforced, in terms of service delivery, by the growth of mixed economies of provision and the need to manage the networks which emerge. Again, this suggests experience in a mixture of settings.

- **New professionalism** — local government has much experience and a justifiably high reputation for its professionals and for the professional strength of its services. A new emphasis on the commissioning role of the local authority highlights the need for a different kind of professional: the professional good at spotting and assessing needs, working with others to seek the best ways of meeting those needs and then at setting standards, monitoring and evaluating provision. And in all this working closely with communities and citizens. The new interest in Continuing Professional Development provides an opportunity to develop new kinds of skills and people.

- **Commissioners and providers** — good management on either side of the divide is important. The key point about commissioning has just been made but is usually ignored in practice. On the provider/contractor side, the tasks of managing within the disciplines of a market or quasi-market, on the end of a contract or formal agreement and on terms defined by the commissioner, are already leading to a new set of managers and managerial careers sometimes even crossing the public–private sector divide. As important are career patterns which will help develop the relationship between the two sides. The need to facilitate learning and to develop strong and flexible relationships between the two sides is critical. It is thus important to develop contractual relations which avoid some of the disadvantages of the 'classic model', build on the strengths of greater mutuality, and at the same time encourage learning. Finding ways of encouraging movement across the divide, so creating both a body of experience and close informal relationships, will foster the creation of trust and close working.

- **Flexibility** — much has been made of the need for greater flexibility and adaptability in both personal and organisational terms. An important part of this is to broaden working experience and involvement in different managerial situation, styles and approaches and to encourage as much learning as possible across boundaries. Different working patterns (job-sharing, part-time working, partnership and joint working, and so on) will also help.

To meet these requirements by developing new career patterns will require imagination and determined action. There are a range of possibilities and moves waiting to be exploited — broadening of careers across departments and organisations, temporary as well as permanent moves, new experience within a job as preparation for a non-traditional move, and so on. The costs of disruption to the status quo should be outweighed by the long term benefits which should begin to flow. Change cannot happen overnight but, step by step, significant transformation should be possible. And, insofar as these steps involve other organisations, they should help in redefining the boundaries of local public management.

Career moves can usefully be thought of in two ways: permanent moves, where the individual becomes contractually committed to a new employing organisation; and temporary ones, where the employer is the same but the job and working situation is new. The latter involve secondment or attachment on a full or part time basis, agreed between organisations short or long term, and working to a clear brief or objective. The first category is easy to think of but difficult to achieve. Deeper considerations — conventional patterns and culture — and apparently more superficial ones, like pension arrangements, easily get in the way.

The second category — secondment and attachment — may offer the best avenue for immediate progress. There are a range of possibilities.

- **Between different parts of the same local authority** — still surprisingly uncommon despite the complexity and variety of what any local authority does.

- **Between neighbouring local authorities** — the possibilities for counties and districts to create arrangements which both enhance their joint working and increase the range of experience available are enormous. Similar possibilities exist among groups of adjacent metropolitan authorities. The creation of new unitary councils might open special possibilities geared to the business of getting the organisation and its services going.

- **Between the organisations involved in local governance** — where joint working is taking place or collaborative effort is needed to develop local strategy or make progress on a major issue and involving public, voluntary and private sectors.

- **Between service providers** — engaged in a local mixed economy of provision (or, of course, between commissioner and provider) helping also to foster long term relationships and learning.

- **Between sectors** — where the objective is as much about gaining new insight or developing new understanding, i.e. central government, private sector management, etc. as management experience.

❏ Management training and development

Changing career patterns will play their part in renewing local public management, albeit that their impact is likely to come in the longer term. There are more immediate possibilities from management training and development. However, demands made on training and management development budgets are usually intense — and there are worrying signs of reduction in the face of spending cuts. There are also indications of a growing unwillingness to allow managers at all levels to have time away from the job. This is perhaps another consequence of fewer people doing more work. Whatever the constraints and demands it is important that the resources and potential available are used to the full.

Training must always have regard for the needs of tomorrow not the demands of yesterday. This will be as important for managers as anyone. The 'curriculum' must be built round the requirements of changing career patterns. The full range of development opportunities (formal training events and courses; seminars and discussion opportunities; conferences; project work; mentoring, coaching and counselling; appraisal and the like) need to drive continuing management renewal.

Wherever possible, opportunities should be taken to promote activities across organisational boundaries — obviously within the authority but, again, between neighbouring councils and between organisations in the locality. Informal contacts built up in this way can be a powerful force in spanning boundaries and developing working relationships. They can also be a way of developing shared understanding about the nature of management in the local public domain and of promoting joint exploration of issues and challenges facing the locality.

Going beyond the general there are then a number of specific issues which need to be noted for the training and development agenda:

- The development and enhancement of skills and competences is important and the new emphasis on the latter is helpful. However, again, the importance of a holistic view of management and organisations must be emphasised. In a very real way good management is more than the sum of its parts. Attention needs to be paid to ways in which the holistic view can be nurtured and developed. Care therefore needs to be taken that training does not rely only on breaking down the management task into separate parts.

- Management development needs to interact closely with career development and support the changing patterns which are needed.

- Training and development activities should provide intellectual stimulus and encourage the search for new ideas and for the challenging and questioning of received wisdom and practice. That is not to say that received wisdom is always wrong, but part of continuing renewal is to continually review.

- Emphasis on the service culture and the importance of seeing organisation and management from the bottom-up needs to be drawn in. It is too easy for training and development to reinforce a top down view by focusing on top down concerns. Opportunities need to be made to draw in people and create situations where the local authority and local governance are seen 'from the street'.

- The demands of constant change and the development of an understanding about the pressures and trends of change in the broader environment will themselves provide subject matter for the curriculum as well as driving it.

In short, management training and development has an important part to play in renewing local public management. It must be used as such and shaped accordingly. There is plenty of rhetoric about developing strategies for management development. The demand now must be to turn these to action, and to act collaboratively and co-operatively, 'thinking local governance' in doing so.

❏ Organisation development

Management training and development activities do not take place in a vacuum. It is essential that they are related to their environment. In other words, they are undertaken to encourage and develop managers and management suited to the objectives and purpose of their organisation. Thus, in turn, **the development of people needs to go hand in hand with the development of the wider organisation, which itself needs careful and explicit attention.** Another obvious point but one often forgotten.

We have touched on a number of aspects of organisation development. These need to be brought together:

- **Change** — change in the environment or purpose of an organisation requires the organisation to change and develop to meet the new circumstances. This is sometimes just left to happen. It should not be so. Preparation, setting a timetable, agreeing who does what and carefully monitoring progress are essential.

- **Community** — the organisation has been likened to a community, demanding and receiving the commitment and involvement of its members. Communities develop and grow but require nurture and support along the way.

- **Strategic management** — a key part of strategic management is delivering a changed organisation. The strategic issues are the ones which will cause the organisation to act in new and different ways which don't fit with the conventional ways of operating. Strategic management is about the process of change. Again, plans need to be laid and preparation made to accommodate the required changes, with the organisation being developed to meet the new circumstances.

- **The service organisation** — one of the most difficult things is to keep an organisation outward looking and customer-focused. Maintaining and developing a service culture requires attention to every aspect of organisational life. It involves constant attention to developing the organisation to make sure it is improving not retreating. In particular, it means a constant effort to see itself from the outside in and to try and build its policy and practice from the bottom up.

- **Governance and community** — 'local governance' and being continually aware of the relationship between the organisation, other actors on the local governmental stage and the community at large. This involves the constant search for processes and structures which can be shaped and developed to make this happen — and to improve them.

- **Fitness for purpose** — all organisations need to be shaped and built to serve a particular set of purposes or direction. As purpose is defined or redefined so the various facets of organisational life require to be shaped and developed to serve that purpose.

Taken together these points emphasise the importance of organisation development for the management agenda. One implication is that organisation development needs not just to be taken seriously, but have responsibility for it clearly defined. The chief executive and her or his senior management colleagues have a key responsibility, but they need support. Special skills and an understanding of organisational dynamics are involved. Some kind of dedicated resource will be needed — at least in an authority of any size. Ideally these should lie with the personnel function and alongside other support activities for human resource management.

The personnel function, incidentally, is part of that shift which has taken place in central support services from control to enabling. People management is a core part of staff and line management, but requires access to specialist support and advice. Some of this is likely to be provided at the centre, but now also tends to be provided through arrangements where the central function is decentralised to departments. However that division is defined, organisation development should be driven from the centre. It is part of the strategic core, acting in support of chief executive and senior colleagues in their strategic tasks. The person or people should be close to (and 'at the right hand' of) those who lead the organisation, working alongside those who are developing the organisation's strategic and corporate capacity. They are part of the same engine of change and development.

❏ Elected members

In talking about people issues it is all too easy to concentrate only on the officer side of the organisation. That is a mistake because:

- political management requires development and elected members require the same kind of support and help as managers;

- the political organisation (structures, processes and people) needs to develop in similar ways;

- strategic management and the delivery of strategic change involves councillors as well as managers;

- there are important issues — and often an unfortunate history — in the way councillors handle officers;

- the need to take the external focus (both in terms of seeing the organisation from the outside and in working co-operatively and collaboratively) is as important for members as officers;

- there are then the whole set of changes in the way local government is now required to work and in its role which demand new patterns of political management.

In short, the training and development of members and the development of *their* organisation is very important. It is often more difficult because the needs may not readily be spotted by the councillors and, by its nature, it cannot be done *to* them by officers. There may even be resistance for fear of further marginalisation or undue officer influence or even brainwashing. There will certainly be a problem about time.

It is important that elected members themselves see their personal and organisational development as important and that a similar approach is developed to their side of the organisation as the officer side. This is likely to involve a wide variety of possibilities. It will include such things as:

- regular review of political management arrangements and their strengths and weaknesses;

- joint discussion with officers and with external organisations who come into contact with the authority's political management about its role and effectiveness;

- joint discussion with officers about roles and relationships and the changes taking place;

- the use of seminars and informal sessions to inform and to explore new issues and ideas;

- programmes of training and development activities to develop skills, knowledge and understanding, not least related to the external role of the councillor in local governance and about how to get the best from the local authority's own organisation;

- definition of the tasks and expectations of councillors and self-evaluation of performance.

As far as possible all of these initiatives and activities should be planned and owned by councillors themselves.

❑ Developing a learning culture

In Chapter 6 we discussed the importance of the learning organisation and described some of its characteristics. **Organisations cannot learn if people do not learn. Part of developing a learning organisation is about developing a culture of learning.** This will be partly to do with training and development and a recognition that personal education, training and development are essential for continuing renewal. But it is more than this. It is about creating an environment in which:

- assumptions can be challenged;

- new ideas and thinking can be explored;

- personal potential and capacity is given room to flourish;

- experience is constantly reviewed and its conclusions fed back into practice;

- where reflection is highly prized not undervalued.

145

The danger is that such things can become a substitute for action. That will not be true of an organisation driven by a true learning culture, where the motive and purpose will be about seeking and delivering improved performance through this learning.

Part of encouraging and developing a learning culture includes understanding the organisation's learning capacity and how 'the way it is' inhibits or enhances that capacity. An audit which establishes the adequacy (or otherwise) of learning processes including:

- the sources of learning in the organisation

- the channels of learning available to be used

- the assimilation processes at work

- the use which is made of the learning and the response to what is learned

will quickly begin to reveal barriers and inhibitions on the one hand and the things which encourage on the other. Some of them will be to do with structure, processes, procedures and systems; others will be to do with less intangible things like values, myths, informal patterns and relationships, communication barriers, stereotypes and caricatures and sources of motivation and de-motivation. It is all these things which together go to make up the culture. A learning culture requires them all to support the reality of learning and emphasises its importance.

A key part of managerial and political leadership is promotion and leadership of a learning culture both through personal and collective example and by challenging and re-shaping those things which can be seen to undermine it. Praising and rewarding individual and collective learning, accepting mistakes and failures (providing they are learned from) and encouraging the diversity, experiment and exploration which is essential to learning are all an important part of this. Equally, an outward looking focus, open exchange with outside organisations and with service users and citizens and the willingness to see how other people and agencies go about their activity will be essential characteristics of the successful learning culture.

❑ Public management and public service

We return to parallel themes which have run through this book. First, that local government and its management are distinctive. The combination of its

- political environment,

- public accountability,

- relationships with citizens *and* service users,

- multiple functions and responsibility,

- democratic base giving it both choice and voice

make it unique. However it is part of something broader. Public service is not *its* sole prerogative. It is shared by others, elsewhere in the public sector, in the voluntary sector and in the private sector. The processes of local governance bring many other people and organisations into the local public arena.

These two points each raise an implication — one of which is specific to local government and one which is broader. For local government, it is important to be clear about its distinctiveness and about the values which underlie its operation. It is important, too, that greater effort is put into articulating these and to making sure that those involved with its work understand, and as far as possible, share them. Many councils ignore this in the induction of new staff and in the continuing training and development of staff and elected members. This is despite the evidence which suggests that people, both on the inside and outside of local government believe the distinctiveness to be important.

The broader point may sound paradoxical. It applies both to the local authority and to the wider arena of local governance. It is important, at the same time, to make less of the boundary between management in different sectors and the sectors themselves. **Different sectors and organisations — particularly public as against private — will have their differences in emphasis and see particular values as being unique to them or at least of greater importance. However, there will be things in common, and the implication of much of what has been said here is that the common ground is growing. The task is now to see how far this extends.**

The mixed economy of provision involves organisations and agencies across public, voluntary and private sectors. They will all have values about

- service,

- quality,

- the people being served and the way they should be treated,

- service users as co-producers in service delivery,

147

and so on. Equally, local governance involves an even wider range of players across all the sectors. Again, there will be values about such things as:

- the public good,

- defining and serving the local public interest,

- ways in which (public) business is done,

- integrity, propriety, etc.

Here too, the question is how far common understandings can be reached and shared. The common ground can only be established as values and ethos are explored and this requires all those involved to be explicit about their own position. There is a particular task for the local authority in encouraging this process among its agents, contractors and collaborators in the mixed economy of provision. Shared understandings will help create this kind of relationships which, for example, are needed to underpin the relational contract.

The search for the extent of common values and understanding will also reveal differences, and that is just as important. Giving a new definition to (local) public management and grasping what is involved in public service requires an understanding of difference as well as similarity. Local public management is undoubtedly broadening its base; part of its renewal should be to strengthen its identity and, in doing so, enhance its capacity to work together effectively in the service of the locality.

HOW TO USE THIS CHAPTER

- Is your organisation a 'people organisation'? What are its hallmarks? How does it show it values people? Would its staff see themselves as members of a community?

- How good are you at 'boundary spanning'? Is the organisation good at spotting and backing 'boundary spanners'? Where are the gaps? Where are the boundary spanners most needed?

- Are there signs of new career patterns emerging in your authority? What is needed? What steps can be taken to produce them?

- Is enough attention given to management development and to organisation development? Are both geared to tomorrow's needs? If not, how can they be changed? and to what?

- Are there development opportunities for elected members? How can these best be encouraged and extended? What are the most important needs and how are they best met?

- Does this all add up to a 'learning culture'? What is missing? Would everyone agree with your perception? Who needs to act? and how?

10

Postscript: pursuing the agenda

The agenda outlined covers a wide ground. Even then, it is inevitably selective and partial. That simply underlines the challenges facing local public management. Of course, in any given situation, some points will be more important than others, some will already be being pursued and some will represent new challenges. Underlying the agenda's presentation are a series of themes — some explicit, some implicit — which relate to its implementation. By way of conclusion it may be helpful to set these out:

- **Diversity** — it is in the nature of local government that it is diverse. One pattern of organisation or approach will not necessarily be right in another place. Pursuing any part of the agenda is thus not to look for uniformity across local government nor is it to look for general (let alone) simple solutions to be applied regardless of circumstance. Organisations are themselves diverse in style or make-up. This is as true of the local authority itself as it is of partner organisations in local governance. Local variety needs to be respected, just as does the plurality of local society.

- **Messiness** — a recurrent theme has been that local society, local governance and the issues which are faced have all become more complex. Relationships between an increasing number of interests, often conflicting, are equally complicated. 'Messiness' is thus a dominant characteristic. This must be accepted it cannot be replaced by traditional ideas of hierarchy and order. The trick is to find ways not just of tolerating but of managing it.

- **Balance** — it could be easy to pursue one part of the agenda, or one particular approach to a part of it, at the expense of others. Inevitably, there has to be some selectivity and concentration, but maintaining a balance and sense of perspective is important. To over-concentrate attention will be to deny the close inter-relationships which exist between organisations, between issues and problems, and between the various parts of the management task. There will be dilemma and tensions, too, which have to be kept in balance.

- **The holistic** — to talk of balance is to draw attention to the need to take a 'whole' view. Whether talking about the local authority's organisation, its management, its relationship with its public or the processes of local governance, to ignore the whole is to miss the point. Leadership and good management are about helping people understand the whole, however difficult that may be.

- **Continuous renewal** — the agenda is explicitly about continuous renewal. This is important. Change, external and internal, is continuing. This demands flexibility and learning. It also requires continuing adaptation. Sometimes adaptation will not be enough and more radical change will be needed to approach or to style an organisation or relationships. Even here, however, the change needs to be set within the evolving pattern of the organisation.

- **Change with the grain** — continuous renewal implies carrying people and organisations with change. In turn, this implies change which, as far as possible, is in tune with the grain of thought and behaviour rather than constantly cutting across it. That is not to say that people and organisations do not have to change their ways. Far from it: but what it suggests is that the task will be easier and the results more effective if adaptation and renewal build on the organisation as it is and in ways which its people will understand.

❑ Further reading

There are many ways of following-up the themes which are captured in the agenda. The following may make useful starting points:

Changing local government and the new local governance

Bozeman, B. (1993) *Public Management*. San Francisco, Josey Bass.

Etzioni, A. (1993) *The Spirit of Community*. New York, Crown.

Osborne, D. and Gaebler, T. (1992) *Re-inventing Government*. Reading (US), Addison Wesley.

Stewart, J. (1995) *Understanding the Management of Local Government* (2nd edn.), London, Pitman Publishing.

Politics and leadership

Bennis, W. and Nannis, B. (1985) *Leaders*. New York, Harper Row.

Rao, N. (1993) *Managing Change: councillors and the new local government*. York, Joseph Rowntree Foundation.

Stewart, J. (1993) *Supporting the Councillor*. Luton, LGMB.

Purpose and Direction

Bartlett, C. and Ghoshal, S. (1994) 'Changing the role of top management: from strategy to purpose'. In *Harvard Business Review*, November–December.

LGMB. (1991) *Strategies for Success*. Luton, LGMB.

Mintzberg, H. (1994) *The Rise and Fall of Strategic Planning*. Hemel Hempstead, Prentice Hall.

Stacey, R. (1990) *Dynamic Strategic Management for the 1990s*. London, Kogan Page.

Organisational matters

Clarke, M. and Stewart, J. (1990) *The Learning Local Authority*. Luton, LGMB.

LGMB. (1993) *Fitness for Purpose*. Luton, LGMB.

LGMB. Forthcoming. *More Than the Sum of the Parts*. Luton, LGMB.

O'Donovan, I. (1994) *Organisational Behaviour in Local Government*. London, Pitman Publishing.

Closer to the people

Beresford, P. and Croft, S. (1993) *Citizen Involvement*. London, Macmillan.

Gaster, L. (1995) *Quality in Public Service*. Buckingham, Open University Press.

LGTB. (1985) *Getting Closer to the Public*. Luton, LGTB.

Normann, R. (1991) *Service Management* (2nd edn.) Chichester, John Wiley.

Commissioning and services

Osborne, D. and Gaebler, T. (1992) *Re-inventing Government*. Reading (US), Addison Wesley.

Plunkett Foundation (1993) *Ownership for Local Authority Services: a guide for policy-makers*, Long Hanborough, Plunkett Foundation.

Schneider, B. and Bowen, D. (1995) *Winning the Service Game*. Boston, Harvard Business School Press.

Walsh, K. (1995) *Public Services and Market Mechanisms*. London, Macmillan.

People

Dilulio, J. (1995) *De-regulating Public Service*. Washington, Brookings Institution.

Fowler, A. (1995) *Human Resource Management in Local Government* (2nd edn.), London, Pitman Publishing.

Newman, J. Forthcoming. *Shaping Organisational Culture*. London, Pitman Publishing.

Ranson, S. and Stewart, J. (1994) *Management for the Public Domain*. London, Macmillan.

Index